M000203782

I read Lucia's book having jus[t] *I'd worked in for almost two* *didn't even realise I needed to* *find a mirror-image job in a n...* *story. I was hooked. I read the second and started to really think. Each story oozes with different personalities. Every account is inspiring, but none of the challenges and struggles that were faced along the way have been hidden or sugar-coated. As I turned the pages, I read nuggets of motivation that came together in the realisation of a new purpose for working-me that feels exciting and liberating, and I can't wait to get started!*

Clare Worsley—HR Executive

X Change *gives great guidance without the waffle.*

David Moseley, Product Marketing Director iManage

A refreshing, non-corporate book packed full of real and inspiring stories about fulfilling career change and the precious secrets learned along the way. A must-read for any mid-lifer starting to wonder whether the time is right to do something different. I read it sat up in bed and couldn't put it down.

Laura Walker, Talent Director, Mid-life Careers Researcher & Consultant

It's been truly refreshing to read for once, after all the books on titans, gurus and billionaires! A tiny, but powerful book based upon quite ordinary people who have had the courage to significantly change their careers whilst approaching midlife.

They were not all aiming to become super rich but rather super happy. The true stories and the tips will motivate those who are no longer fulfilled by their current jobs and those who are aiming for more in the coming 20 years of their lives.

David Vrba, Partner at Company Culture Market and Digiskills

X Change *will ensure you don't waste another minute of your precious life. If there is one book you need to read this year, make it* **X Change** *and fast track a happier you!*

Marie Claire de Grouchy, CEO WellAT

X Change *is both deeply thought provoking and action provoking*

It's a practical guide to help us manoeuvre around many of the real and perceived obstacles, challenges and excuses that can keep you trapped in an unhappy job all the way to an early grave.

Lucia's approach is not based on an idealistic Hollywood-style impulse to throw away all that you have built so far on a longshot gamble, but rather on a clear, rational, realistic plan formed from deep thought, thorough research and perhaps an element of calculated risk-taking.

A very good investment in yourself that only asks a couple of hours to read and reflect on what you really can change for the better, but one that I will revisit again and again.

Oliver Holt, Interim Commercial Finance Director

This book will inspire you to take steps to regain control of your own destiny and get off the hamster wheel before it's too late... [It] will inspire change in your mindset and allow you to face your fears and move forward.

Craig Aitken, Engineer EDF

We only get one go at this thing called life and none of us are coming out of it alive. Lucia has captured the essence of today's working environment and mixed it with true stories of individuals who have reshaped their careers to make sure that they are striving to make each day as purposeful and rewarding as possible. I loved this book.

Tom Fender, Investor & Director, Multiple Businesses

X Change *is a reminder to all of us that while we might be successful when we focus our skills on the requirements of the job, the magic really happens when we focus those skills on our passions—and it's never too late to make that career change.*

Warren Price, CFO B2M Solutions & CFO/Co-founder Click Labs

Such a great insight into the challenges that so many people face and how they can be overcome.

Selina Lamy, Founder Red Moon Coaching

X Change

How to:

- ☑ Torch your work treadmill

- ☑ Retire your boss

- ☑ Dump the ingrates

- ☑ Torment the passive-aggressives

- ☑ Escape the toxic office

- ☑ Get your fierce on

- ☐ And design the career that lets you live, love and laugh after 40

Lucia Knight

You lovely friend Sarra

Thought you might appreciate

this little book of career hope . . .

Because life's too short to do work

that doesn't feel great.

Jonathan H

The mPowr Legacy

Every moment of your life has the potential to be more
than every moment of your life. As you invest each day
into something greater than yourself—lasting longer than
your lifetime, influencing those yet to be born—you create
a legacy. A legacy that serves others beyond the minutes,
hours and years you will ever spend on Earth. The mPowr
Publishing mission is to inspire your legacy—to help you
create it through the books and media you develop. Every
title we publish is more than the sum of its parts, with
deeper impact, broader transformation and, at its heart, a
legacy that is yours in this moment, right now.

"I want to look back on the next twenty years with less regret than I do the last twenty years."

"I hear this voice telling me to find something different, but I've invested so much time and life energy in this industry… I'm just not sure."

"I feel like I am moving further and further away from work that I really enjoy."

"What the hell am I doing here? I want to do wonderful creative things like I used to. I want to be my own person again."

"I haven't learned anything new for such a long time and somehow that has become very important to me."

"I've hit my mid-forties and have begun to wonder how I want to spend my remaining working career."

"I have, sort of, lost faith in the corporate life."

"I just want *more* from my work."

"I can see what's happening in my company and industry. I just want a great Plan B."

"I'm not unhappy but… that's not enough any more."

For...

Mum and Dad

Erin and Aine

Contents

SECTION 3—Rewriting Your Future Story

SECTION 1

Our Backstory

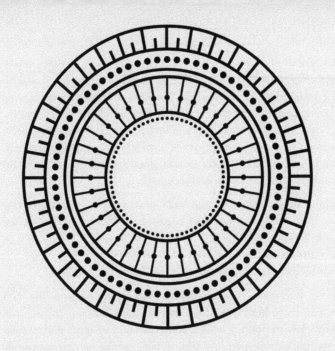

The Light at the End of Our Tunnel

Generation X careers are complicated.

We have found ourselves sandwiched between the fortunate baby boomers, whose pensions have benefited from long, stable careers and the high, some might say, self-entitled expectations of the millennials who rally against our just-do-it work culture.

Generation X has a unique view of the working world—as we should—we radically changed it. The rebellious waves of our youth saw us demanding more dynamism from our careers and lives than was usual in previous generations.

We created opportunities. Opportunities for us to have it all.

Not the baby boomer's view of having it all. That view included high-growth economies, affordable homes, secure incomes, long-term employment, substantial pensions and retirements spent enjoying the fruits of their labour.

The have-it-all world where families needed double incomes to pay the burdensome school and childcare costs of our late-start families, alongside immense mortgages. The have-it-all world that saw us creating and then competing against flexible, global workforces for our next roles. The have-it-all world of caring for those elderly baby boomers at exactly the same time as helping our children grow up. The have-it-all world where technology transformed our work and working environments beyond recognition.

But just because we designed and initiated the biggest technology revolution the globe has ever experienced, doesn't mean we are totally at ease with that technology or its impacts. Certainly not as comfortable as the millennials who integrated our technology into their childhoods and evolved into tech-dependent adults.

Those technology advancements mean that we are the first generation to have almost no idea of which jobs our children will grow up to perform. Even the cornerstone of society's professional roles—doctors, lawyers and accountants—are being unrecognisably transformed by artificial intelligence, which we invented.

Generation X career values have also dramatically altered in line with changes in society.

For instance, our parents' generation rewarded long tenure with one company. Characteristically, we rebelled against that stability and instead rewarded short-term job moves. In fact, that was how many of us progressed our careers, increasing our salaries with each move, while those who remained within one business were punished by receiving only small salary increments. We also evolved our workplaces to include interim and temporary positions as a demonstration of our love of dynamism.

This shorter-term emphasis on our careers, spawned the huge growth of a new industry. There was little need for recruitment businesses in the baby boomer world, yet the global expansion of the recruitment industry from small, local businesses to FTSE 250 and Fortune 500 businesses over a few short decades, offers further evidence of our love for career dynamism.

Our seemingly insatiable drive towards achievement has been underpinned and strengthened by our remarkably strong work ethic. That powerful combination allowed us to change our world spectacularly in a short space of time.

Not all for the better.

Despite technology advancements, we have seen our commuting times and working hours elongate beyond imagination. We now carry our never-ending work home with us, in our pockets and even sleep with it under our pillows.

Our generation evolved our idea of work into something way beyond its bill-paying function. For many of us, work now forms the bedrock of our identities and contributes enormously to our feelings of self-worth. That isn't going to change for us.

For that reason, we cannot leave our careers in the hands of anyone but ourselves. We cannot trust anyone else to care for them as we can.

We must evolve our personal working scenarios in the same way that we evolved our idea of work. Into something that has much deeper potential. Work that has the potential to enrich our lives as we are performing it.

Otherwise, there might not be much light at the end of our tunnel.

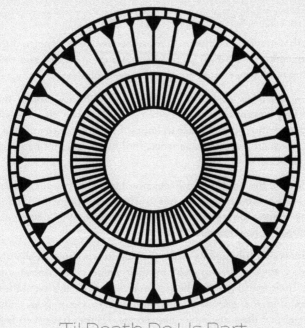

Til Death Do Us Part

Could you keep doing the work that you are currently doing for the next twenty years?

So many of us are waking up in our forties or fifties, lifting our heads up from the daily grind and wondering if we can keep doing what we have been doing for much longer.

Even if our parents didn't love their work, they could just plough on, keeping their eyes fixed firmly on their (comparatively young) retirement age, when they could enjoy many nonworking, hopefully healthy, decades.

The reality, for most of us, will play out very differently.

One thing is for sure—we will work until we are much older than our parents were when they stopped.

Many of us will never experience what we now know as *retirement,* as we will be working far into our seventies—possibly to our graves. There is very little light at the end of a tunnel that involves doing work that doesn't feel fulfilling, satisfying or even enjoyable for *that* long.

With that in mind, it appears to me to be *even* more important that we do work that we love. Or at least put a great deal of effort into figuring out how we could do work that we might love.

This would allow us to live our lives well—*right now,* rather than sacrificing a great deal of life's promise until we can afford to stop doing work that doesn't make us happy. Especially since many of us know, through personal experience, that our lives might be shorter than we hope.

As you read this book, you will feel driven to build changes into your work to taste more of what life has to offer today, rather than waiting for the vague promise of something more or something different in ten, fifteen or twenty years.

The trials and tribulations of the individuals who have deliberately returned to the driving seat of their careers are documented here. Their lows have not been sugar-coated, as this would have understated the discomfort that appears to accompany career change, as it does any major life change. Neither have their highs been dampened. You will see real quotes from each individual on how it feels for them to wake up knowing that they have done the right thing.

Their personal insights and *aha* moments translate into what is required for you to build more satisfaction and more fun into your work. After stepping wholeheartedly into each of their shoes for a few moments, you will also get a tangible sense of the potential positive impacts of making either small tweaks or big changes in your own career.

The secrets you will discover will give you what you need to begin to design your career in such a way that you could keep working happily for as long as you want, rather than for as long as you need.

Imagine yourself potentially working until your grave. If the work that you are currently doing does not make that prospect seem joyous or happy, this book will help you change that.

SECTION 2

X Changing Stories

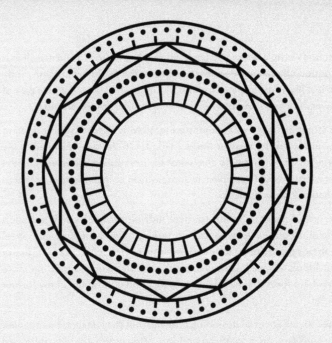

The Secret Keepers

I'd love to introduce you to some of the most ordinary people I have ever met. They also happen to be some of the most deeply inspiring individuals I have had the pleasure of sharing time with.

They have not launched airlines or global music businesses. They have not invented the next Facebook, nor a cure for its overuse. Their faces do not adorn the front covers of magazines or newspapers. They don't even quote themselves on Instagram.

They are the sort of individuals who have a supportive and fun friendship group that they don't see often enough. They try hard to do enough exercise. They occasionally have a tired twitchy eye that no one else can see but they announce it to everyone in case they are accused of winking provocatively. And when they were young, they watched way too much tv and can quote lines from Die Hard, Cheers or The Wonder Years. And hum the theme tunes from Cagney and Lacey or The A-Team at the drop of a hat.

But the reason I feel inspired by them is that they designed happier careers for themselves. And that is no mean feat.

It sounds simple when you say it quickly but when I found myself in a situation where I wanted to do just that, the world around me made me feel like I was hoping to climb Mount Everest armed with a pair of flowery flip flops and a set of fluffy ear-muffs. Utterly stupid.

So stupid in fact that I committed to an MSc Psychology, imagining I would learn the answer there. I didn't. On the day I handed in my dissertation, with still no clue what my next career move would be, I *knew* that I would specialise in some way in career change... *because it shouldn't be this difficult!*

From that point, I began to meet individuals from our generation who shared their experiences of getting behind the steering wheel of their careers after letting it self-drive for a while. Very ordinary individuals whose journeys to doing happier work taught me more about life than the 3000+ interviews I had conducted in my former career.

Their experiences of designing careers, that they describe as *happier*, *more fulfilling*, *more satisfying* and very often *more enjoyable*, intrigued and inspired me so much that it became my mission to learn how they did it.

However, none of them could articulate all of their secrets consciously. But I knew if I met enough individuals, who described themselves as happier after redesigning their work, that their secrets could not evade me for long.

By asking the right questions to enough of them, I knew that I could extract whatever shared wisdom, hidden know-how or mystical superpowers they possessed. I could find out what lay beneath their ability to design happier careers for themselves.

By jumping into the shoes of each of these very ordinary, yet inspiring individuals for just a few minutes, you too will appreciate the secrets buried deep within them. The secrets that offered them the magic to allow them to unstick their own careers.

I encourage you to pause after every couple of stories to unlock their secrets in a way that makes sense to you.

The earlier you understand their secrets and begin to apply them to your own situation, the earlier you too will be able to stop wasting your precious time doing work that you don't love.

14

Radio for Inspiration

Kate

Aerospace and defence executive to gin maker

For some individuals, their desire to change career is prompted by a seemingly random occurrence, a conversation with a stranger or something as simple as a snippet from a radio or tv show. If it catches them at the right moment, in the right frame of mind, it can spark an idea that either dissolves or can be engineered to take flight. Kate had one such experience from which her new career soared.

The name's Bombed... Kate Bombed.

Kate had racked up more hours with her hands on the controls of combat aircraft simulators than most RAF pilots. From an early age, she had aimed her target at the defence and aerospace sectors and had loved the thrills and spills of bringing inventive, undercover ideas to fruition.

When she jetted into the intrigue and copious gin martinis of the private sector, her experience and energy around all things new-found her heading up the global innovations team at Q branch, from secret locations. Children added to the buzz, making home life advance at a new pace. The two lives intermingled beautifully.

As her eldest started school, she handed over her wings to return home to England but kept leading her gadget-driven team. All was well for a while but soon the gentle wheels of commerce had begun to leave her need for speed and her creative juices somewhat unsated.

One memorable commute set her creative heart afizz.

En route to the airport to attend a board meeting, Kate tuned into a radio show on the international gin renaissance which had instigated a boom in gin microdistilling.

Before the show had ended, bubbles of excitement had embedded themselves in the deep dark depths of her stomach. They bounced around her body touching brain and toes simultaneously.

Kate *knew,* in that instant, that she would set up a gin microdistillery.

She dialled for a collaborator, "Helen, I've an important assignment for you. I need you to trust me." By the end of the call, she had convinced fellow gin lover and great friend Helen to join the gin making explosion. Initially, for their eyes only.

By the time she stepped onto her plane, Kate knew three things: how to make gin, the required equipment and the major players in the premium gin market. By the time she exited the plane she'd also sketched out a rough business plan. She worked faster than a speeding bullet.

Later, over gin, shaken *and* stirred, the business research project took off like a fast Aston Martin from Plymouth to London.

Viability. Market gaps. Timing. Costs. Projections.

Even later, the real-life research.

Acceptable sacrifices? Time needed? Energy levels? Family support? Financial investment? Skills?

Kate and Helen decided their mission, and they chose to accept it, was to make the finest gin in the world.

With one big *but*.

They could risk nothing. Both had children. Both had substantial mortgages. There would, however, be heavy investments of a different kind.

Their free time. Their non-sleeping hours. Their weekends. And their evenings. These would be the weighty investments.

In the meantime, they would carry on as normal. Full-time positions with their undercover side hustle, learning as much as they could about gin.

No need for Q's high-tech devices, they built their microdistillery with a refreshingly simple list of gadgets. A still, some base alcohol and a range of botanicals.

They packed their nonworking, waking hours with gin chemistry experiments for months on end.

Skills and confidence mounted until the day when invitations were extended to a big group of gin-loving mummy friends to a memorable kitchen party.

A blind, gin-tasting kitchen party.

Unguided and unprompted, their handcrafted gins were sipped dry while the market-leading premium gins lingered.

That was the moment they both *knew* that their gin kitchen would work. It would be the route to their lives, well lived. Filled to the brim with creativity. Bunged with herby, joyful moments and mini celebrations.

And shared fun.

They would squeeze the zest from their lives in the form of their business. They would seek out new talents and learn the unknown while tapping into their vibrant community. They would do it together, trusted friends with complementary skills and personalities. They would enjoy the journey no matter where it ended. They would live and let dry... gin.

They were granted their first licence to inebriate by a local bar and launched their first gin. Soon that gin was stocked by a few local bars and shops. When it sold out and reorders were received, more and more venues joined The Gin Kitchen team. Their confidence reached such heights that they pitched their first gin to Fortnum and Mason's spirit buyer.

He offered them Spirit of the Month twice that year. They declined the first as they couldn't make enough stock in time but on the second, they sold out... twice.

Kate's experiment has gone so far beyond that little bubble of excitement in her stomach. The Gin Kitchen has moved to bigger premises and she now spends 100% of her working time there.

Kate transformed from free-time gin maker to full-time gin maker in a few short years.

This career change story will self-destruct in five seconds.

When I interviewed Kate in her first premises, a tiny freezing outhouse at the back of her local pub, she was wearing a cosy woolly jumper, not a scrap of make-up and was testing a new recipe. When I took her photo for my records, I described her as "shining with happiness". Here's how she described how her new career makes her feel.

"It feels great being creative all day. Being involved in everything. Gin distilling, label design, launch planning, marketing, operations and delivery all involve creativity. Even the seemingly boring elements like risk assessment or designing the processes behind 5* food hygiene ratings feel creative.

We feel happy, proud and confident in what we have produced and we are having such a lot of fun along the way."

The Secret Diary of a 49½-Year-Old

Martine

European HR Director to franchise owner of local HR consultancy.

For some, our definition of success changes as we grow older. In our youth, many of us aimed for that jet set lifestyle, the designer suits, international travel, an expense account or a business card with an impressive-sounding title. Signals to the world that we have arrived. As we gain a few wrinkles, our sense of what is important appears to shift towards the less tangible rewards in life. Martine redesigned her career to prioritise more of those intangible, but increasingly crucial, elements in her life.

She would turn 50 in less than a year.

50. Half a century. A good vintage.

The first vintage when women could have it all.

began to contemplate her next moves, Martine paused to
her her achievements to date.

Viewed from the outside, boxes were being ticked.

Two wonderful daughters with her lovely husband. Tick.

A beautiful home. Tick.

Multi-country HR strategies designed. Multiple successful site relocations to Eastern Europe. Sponsored to join Harvard High Potentials Leadership Programme. Tick. Tick. Tick.

Viewed from the inside, a few knots had appeared.

The weekly dawn date with Heathrow's Terminal 5 had grown tiresome. Her boss's desire to constantly showboat her and her HR team around Europe clashed severely with her own personal style. The increasingly tangled world of politics over people had worn thin.

Worn almost bare.

The never-ending grafting to create work-life balance had lost momentum alongside the disappearing connection to the purpose of her work. The years of fine-tuning multiple diaries and time zones so as not to miss birthdays, parent evenings and performances had left her fraying at the edges.

Only one event had fallen through the cracks but almost no one remembered that sports day.

That's when Martine decided to design her own list of boxes. And to stop ticking someone else's.

She pulled on the thread she sensed had been luring her home and two young teenage girls tugged back on it. They wanted her at home. They needed her at home.

She wanted to be there for them. She needed to be there for them.

But she also needed to design more fulfilling work. For herself.

Her almost 50-year-old self.

20

The precisely managed timetable of relentless planes, trains and tuk-tuks had taken its toll on Martine's health and fitness.

As she looked at her reflection, her physical appearance wasn't as she'd hoped it would be on the runway to her fiftieth birthday.

Over the last few years, squeezing in gym trips before or after multi-country trips had ground to a halt. Tiny body changes had gone unnoticed but, in that moment, she challenged herself to enter her new vintage in much better shape. She discovered the art of high intensity interval training.

One new personal box to tick.

Next.

It didn't take long to figure out that the constant planes, trains and Apple Martinis was a lifestyle box that she would erase.

Her lofty rank had excluded her from HR on the ground, which was historically the really fulfilling part of her mid-career. She set about learning what she needed to know to set up her own HR business, her way.

The timing felt right. The imminent arrival of that big birthday hinted at a last chance.

A now-or-never moment.

There was so much to learn. She chose the franchise model to enter the competitive local HR market to give her the greatest chance for a successful opening year. She would receive help with marketing, finance and social media so that she could concentrate on the unveiling of a Martine-styled HR consultancy.

So that's what she did. She designed her new career. Tick.

Next.

Martine's story of recognising which aspects of her working life she didn't want and which she did, formed the foundation of her career overhaul. Consciously designing work around the elements she enjoyed and then interweaving those amongst other important life priorities made her successful career change possible. When I met Martine, I wondered how it felt for her to entwine work and life more fluidly. This was what she told me.

"No fancy benefits package will ever compensate me for the time I am having with my children since starting my own business. If I hadn't done what I did, I know I would have regretted it. I was able to help my daughter through her GCSEs successfully. If I'd been in my old life, I would not have been able to be here for her as much as I was able to. I would have felt guilty for not being here.

When a client, who has recognised that they need help, takes my advice, experiences a positive outcome and then thanks me, I wish I could bottle that feeling and sprinkle it around the world!"

If She Always Does
What She Always Did

Liz

Teacher to micro-baker

Things don't always have to hit a tipping point of pain to force change. Some successful career changers are so inspired by a new experience that they develop it into a defining moment—a watershed point between their historical and future careers. Liz spoke with me about the unexpected new experience that she built into her defining moment.

The smell of little handmade biscuits turning golden in the oven was a fading but well-tended memory in Liz's house. Her little-handed bakers were all grown up now and had left home.

As a primary school teacher, there was never any shortage of mini-bakers eager to bake sticky, sweet treats, but it wasn't the same. She still enjoyed teaching but longed for something *more*. Sadly, she could never really put her finger on what that *more* might look like. Her dream was to do something in the food industry but again she drew a blank around the potential specifics.

When she'd almost forgotten about searching for her *more*, an advertisement caught her eye. A course in *How to Set Up a Micro-bakery*.

Why not? She'd done a little bread baking but historically it was in those sticky treats that her skills shone.

How different could it be? How different indeed.

While creating her first loaf, she'd accessed the special kind of magic bread making could offer her. The pureness of the ingredients. The meditative kneading that cleared the mind. The movement. The control. Mindful magic.

As the course progressed, she got to know her fellow mindful magicians through the kneading process and discovered a common bond. They were all in transition.

Gingerbread women who had been flattened by the uniformity of their cookie-cutter worlds.

Wishing to add new spices to their life recipes.

Craving the celebration of their long-forgotten or yet-to-be-discovered, misshaped edges.

Creating something so wonderful from almost nothing was helping each of them. Liz had found her new clan, one that fit her just perfectly.

She'd also been walloped over the head by a giant dough ball.

It had ignited an obsession within her that she hadn't known existed. Ever. The obsession crept through her purpose-filled hands and seeped under her skin.

Recipes were googled. Books sourced. Articles read. Programmes consumed. And bread of course! Bread was baked. And baked. And baked.

This was what *more* felt like to Liz.

Whilst she continued her teaching part-time, the obsession dug its floury claws deeper. She volunteered in bakeries and cooking schools

24

to learn every morsel there was to learn about bread making. Being around kitchens as the washer-upper meant that she could just be in kitchens, watching, listening and absorbing.

Over time, her helpfulness and curiosity led to conversations with the bakers and chefs about her new love. Over time those conversations led to helping out with the actual baking in professional kitchens. Always learning.

After the micro-bakery course ended, she decided to continue studying to become a nationally accredited Bread Angel.

But building the confidence to sell that first loaf took much longer than Liz had imagined. Friends and family were always complimentary but her fear that her bread wasn't good enough to sell commercially was holding her back.

She needed validation from people in the know. So, nervously she offered her bread up to be judged at the World Bread Awards UK and was delighted to be selected as a runner-up. Confidence sorted. Liz sold her first loaf.

And her little business began to rise.

She spent her free time practising hundreds of recipes and delivering her goods directly to the doors of her grateful customers—at an unspecified time on the promised day. A little boost of local PR meant that the business grew slowly but surely until the time she could resign from her teaching role and create her own special signature style of magic on a full-time basis.

Liz then needed to point her learning towards the business behind the bread making. She began to do tutorials, webinars and courses on social media marketing, accounting, packaging, PR and photography.

Others might have found that draining but it completely energised her as she cared so much about making her product the best it could be.

A little later in her baking business journey, Liz combined her years of teaching experience with her micro-baking know-how to train others how to set up their own micro-bakeries.

To sprinkle bread making magic far and wide.

When I caught up with Liz, I wanted to know if any of that early magic had worn off. See for yourself.

"Baking is a slow form of therapy. There is magic in the process. I feel joyful. I love teaching people to bake—it can be transformational. It comes from the heart. I love bringing joy into other people's lives.

I walk downstairs to work. I can have a day off when I want to. I feel blessed. I deliver to my customers sometime in the afternoon so there's no time pressure. Most days I think—am I really doing this AND getting paid for it?"

A Hospital Room
with a View

Jennifer

PA to social media trainer

Quite often, career change is preceded by a dramatic event that forces us to rip the blinkers from our eyes and to review our life as a whole. The good, the bad and the ugly. If work floats to the very top of the problem list, action is necessary. In this instance, the dramatic event was a life-changing back injury that brought everything else into perspective. When we met, Jennifer relived the event that began an irreversible shift in her relationship with her work.

Waiting to be wheeled off to the operating theatre, Jennifer indulged in a rare moment of reflection on life over the last few years. She then tried to imagine a future without pain.

Despite her fear of going under the knife, the dream of pain-free walking, sitting and standing couldn't hinder the arrival of a hopeful smile. But that smile was cut short by the incessant beeping of her phone signalling incoming messages from her team.

Simple requests. Lazy requests. Where to find such and such a folder? How to do such and such a task? Could she just do one last little thing before she went on her break?

Jennifer would have gladly responded to all their requests if *even one* of them had offered a tiny morsel of empathy for her scary road ahead.

Would it have been too much effort to send a tiny bunch of flowers? To sign a card? To whizz off a rushed email wishing her a speedy recovery? Did her hard work and loyalty over more than a decade matter to any of them?

Not a single one of them had even said "Good luck."

Several years and a great deal of effort had been expended in an attempt to avoid this risky back surgery following a painful slipped disc.

Into an already hectic schedule, Jennifer had squeezed nearly 70 physiotherapy appointments over a two-year period. Four epidurals also turned out to be necessary when the painkillers stopped taking the edge off her agony.

But they weren't enough.

A few days before Christmas, with all the shopping done and most of her year-end work complete, Jennifer awoke in such crippling pain that she couldn't stand upright. That morning, the years of intensive pain management culminated in Jennifer begging her doctor to authorise the only option they hadn't yet tried. He'd finally agreed.

The necessary surgery was booked for that chilly January morning when Jennifer found herself contemplating her future to the soundtrack of email and voicemail notifications.

She paused to wonder, *If I die today, would I die happy?* The negative response pointed directly at the troublesome, broken piece of her life's jigsaw.

Work.

There was no denying that Jennifer felt needed by everyone at work. But, she couldn't recall a time when she'd felt appreciated.

She really *wanted* to feel more appreciated. She *needed* to feel more appreciated.

Riding off to theatre under a cloud of disappointment, she resolved to make some changes.

Two months of lying flat on her back staring at the ceiling was just what the doctor ordered.

With nothing to do but heal, the minutes bled into hours. The hours into days. Days into weeks. Weeks to months. Something had to change. Something big. But how? And then, of course, when?

Intermingling endless box sets with visits from near and dear and deep thinking about her work situation, Jennifer uncovered two specific problems requiring attention.

One.

The bonuses.

She had allowed her ample annual bonuses to build their own financial prison around her life.

Her industry-standard large bonuses were viewed as the holy grail of a successful career by family and friends in Ireland. Giving them up would be considered as mind-losing behaviour.

Every year, there had been some short-term financial goal to stick around for—a new kitchen or a special holiday. The realisation hit home hard. These bonuses were tethering her to a role and an organisation that didn't fit her any more, and perhaps never did.

Two. Everything else!

Flat on her back, Jennifer felt like she had awakened from an eleven-year career coma. The cloud had lifted. With clearer vision than she had possessed for quite some time, she realised her boss didn't value her input. Neither did her team. So, what on earth was she doing there?

The decision was made. Her future would be found elsewhere. She would begin to nurture a droplet of a plan... just as soon as she had dealt with some unfinished business.

On her return to work, Jennifer resolved to do everything she could to find ways to satisfy her craving to feel more appreciated, however short term.

She applied for and won various industry awards. She was crowned the Most Networked PA in London and won a Super Achiever Global Pitman Training award. Appreciation felt as satisfying as she had hoped and spurred on her efforts to overhaul her career.

The more practical elements of the plan began to emerge slowly during her staged re-entry to work.

Building work that she could enjoy more and serving a more appreciative customer base formed the foundational elements of the plan. Remarkably, the skills Jennifer had used to win those awards formed the basis of her career's new direction. When the plan was nearly ready, she resigned and stepped back into the driving seat of her career.

Jennifer now uses a lifetime of skills—including her English degree, her love of connecting people and her enjoyment of teaching—to deliver social media marketing training for entrepreneurs.

When we caught up, I was curious how Jennifer would answer the *If I died today, would I die happy?* question now. Here's how she responded.

"I would say yes because I would die knowing that I was truer to myself, that I was valued and definitely felt respected. It feels so good to be of value and to be appreciated for helping others to do something they couldn't do without me.

By training the individuals behind companies to do their own social media marketing, I feel like I am increasing their confidence. I can make a difference to them and their businesses. It's exciting!"

The Long Walk from Futility

Andy

International finance director to founder of his accounting firm

Sometimes, when the work that we do moves away from work that feels authentic and purposeful, it can begin to feel like a performance. These feelings can be exacerbated by stressful working routines that clash with wider life desires. If this goes on for too long, a motivational shift occurs which either prompts us to do something about it or to renegotiate with ourselves to accept the situation forever. Andy chose to do the former.

The 4.30am alarm buzzed, the conductor's baton tapping to alert the orchestra to the opening piece of the opera, *Andy's Working Week*.

No need. Andy was awake and alert. He'd been rehearsing the lyrics for his upcoming performance since the wee small hours. Worrying about missing his flight. Agonising about the impact of his presentation. They'd heard his aria before, but he wanted to impress the new members of the board audience, to give the critics a good show.

On the well-trodden taxi route to whichever airport, in whatever country, he prepared to present the dancing profit and loss numbers. Comparing them against a forgotten global target for a range of unmemorable consumer products.

As he stared out of the car window on a stunning, summer Sunday afternoon, he considered how much of his life he'd spent travelling. How much of his free time he had spent on tour performing similar numbers to increasingly argumentative, challenging and aggressive board audiences.

Glancing at his performance schedule, he estimated that 50% of his life over the last decade had been spent far away from his home country.

For what cause?

At what cost?

It all felt so dramatically necessary, yet futile.

His booming lead tenor voice, the extraordinary hero of the opera, had begun to sound somewhat strained.

Strained by his daily scan of newspapers searching for rumours that his company was to be acquired. In recent years, just keeping track of the name of his company had become a task in itself. Filling him with deep baritone warnings to "Beware." It had happened before and would happen again. Hostile, overnight takeovers had become the norm.

In his consumer world, companies were being devoured by companies, who later devoured other companies. Impossible to figure out heroes or villains. But the audiences seemed to love the drama of the giant family feuds, the mergers and the acquisitions.

Andy shared the stage with a huge cast of 40-something directors. Upstarts who all gazed up towards the turrets of stage-right castles to watch the revered, bearded leaders in their fifties. Eagerly awaiting their fall from grace. Before scrambling upwards, knives at the ready, to take their spots in the limelight.

Que sera sera.

Except the 50-something leaders endured, clinging to the stage theatrically, reluctant to take their leave. Thinking their stage presence was everlasting.

But the slavering lions in the boardroom were hungry for Christian flesh. The junior cast members starving and eager for their lead positions. Scrambling to suck on the miniscule morsels of meat on bones discarded by their seniors.

He'd had enough.

He was ready for a stage-left exit.

He needed a break from the rigmarole. Something less of a performance, less melodramatic, more real. Something where honesty trumped powerful-voiced lions in the boardroom and baying shareholders.

Alone on the set, orchestra hushed, Andy redrew his options.

Working for another big company with their boardroom performances was a no go. They were all the same. His days of performing on a global stage were over. He'd grown tired of being directed and of being boxed in. He needed to cut all ties from those corporate stages. He craved freedom to work in his way, where he pleased and how he pleased. He decided to put his training to good use but to point his financial talents in a different direction.

He kept working on a part-time basis but accepted a diminished role to bankroll his new idea.

In the meantime, he learned lots of little new skills. Skills that he'd never needed on the global stages.

He decided to help small businesses run their finances. To help them make their businesses stronger. He started spreading the news in the streets, the gyms and coffee shops. He swapped arias in big corporations for bit parts in small businesses, lots of them.

The curtain came down at the end of his first year, to rapturous applause from new customers and his family. He allowed himself a little bow.

When Andy and I caught up, he had left the dramatic opera of big corporates several years earlier. He was still revelling in his rejuvenated enjoyment of doing valuable work and feeling valued by clients. He appeared not to miss any elements of his old life, so I wondered about the differences between his previous and new career.

"A major difference is that I see my kids more. For so many years I left before they went to school and I'd return when they were in bed. Or I would travel the world for two weeks at a time.

I love my work now. I learned that I am never going to retire. I'm going to be carried out in a box."

We've Come a Long, Long Way Together

Lindsay

Banking sales and marketing executive to wine entrepreneur

For some career changers, not being unhappy is simply not enough. These individuals usually don't experience one single trigger for change. Instead, they feel the need to collect a body of evidence, clue by clue, until they can make the decision to change. They accumulate a multitude of signals that point them away from their current direction and even more signals to reveal other possible new directions. At some point, the evidence guides them in a direction that energises them. That's when things begin to pick up pace.

Midnight. An elegantly refined evening of delectable dining and fine wine drew to a close. The boisterous and witty conversations began to lull and wane, comfortably relaxing towards the evening's end. Clients, still dressed to kill, edged towards the softly lit foyer, whispering their thanks and next time promises.

ul of respected and favoured colleagues remained. A last cap, a time-honoured tradition. They withdrew to relax at their ourite table in the cosy corner of the familiar lounge. The calm and the hush washed over them as they closed in for subdued, late-night discussions.

Until the moment the bombshell was dropped upon Lindsay. A well-liked and highly regarded colleague launched his grenade question. The accidental explosion that signalled death to her first career.

"So, what's *your* Plan B, Lindsay?"

Deceptively innocent. No malicious intent.

Caught unaware.

The pointed inquiry released a tiny violet droplet of truth serum into an otherwise refined career plan. Colour spread ominously into dark corners of her mind, forcing attention on thoughts that had lain untouched for years. Bringing each in to focus.

Exposing concealed truths, one clue at a time. To help her move forward.

The inky venom encircled her career choice. Not a choice so much as one decision. One decision that spawned countless others.

Lindsay, with the long-term planning skills of her twenty-one-year-old self, had tripped and fallen into a graduate scheme in the City. There she initiated her ascent up the steep corporate ladder, taking on bigger teams and running bigger projects in various institutions of merit.

Then the toxic venom began to corrupt her. It strangled the truth from her with the stealth of Mrs Peacock, in the billiard room, with the rope.

The venom leached across her industry. An industry where careers were murdered day after day, so often it had begun to appear normal. The horror of the constant news of career fatalities, seeped furtively into homes across the country, devastating thousands of families in private. But not before publicly televising their shame of being ejected from their offices holding their career ashes in rain-splashed, ready-made cardboard boxes.

Decision made, she had gone as far as she wanted in that industry.

Peering closer without her rose-tinted glasses, Lindsay realised that a board position held no interest. Her promotions had done nothing but move her further away from her two true loves: working directly with clients and negotiating deals.

Although the violet venom had unveiled many truths, it hadn't revealed any future answers. Lindsay began to collect her future clues by herself and started with her life outside work.

Wine came to mind. She had always wanted to learn more and would love to weave wine into work somehow. Mystified, she hunted for her elusive Plan B, and decided to learn more about wine in the meantime.

She and her husband had done a few evening courses for fun ten years ago and she itched to learn more. She signed up to study for a Wine and Spirits Education Diploma—a degree level course—scary, but just what she needed.

She wedged her sparkling new tasting glasses under one arm and left the office every Monday at 6.30pm over the next year and a half, while pondering that elusive Plan B. Diploma in hand, it still eluded her but her love for wine had grown.

Meanwhile the evidence had stockpiled against her old career. Her interest in riding another repeated annual cycle plummeted to rock bottom.

A redundancy opportunity stepped forth, an identity parade of sorts. A hand-raising opportunity to exit the industry. She raised her hand, it was shaken and they agreed her exit.

With *still* no Plan B, she decided to spend her redundancy package investigating. Lindsay donned her deerstalker hat, her microscope and notebook and embarked on a year-long, investigative tour of the wine industry.

Clues were inspected up and down the country. She visited every wine cellar she could and attended every advertised wine fair. She interviewed wine company owners on their experiences. She met distributors and retailers every week. Questioning and quizzing all through that year. Never knowing when she might need the knowledge.

Until the big reveal.

She'd fallen in love with this new industry.

What she'd found was a refreshing and positive industry. Optimistic and accessible. Honest and transparent. And unusually open to new entrants. The opposite mentality to the cut-throat, closed, tight industry that she'd spent her first career in.

When the push came to shove, she was ready. She had learned so much from the real stories of wine business owners that her business plan came easily. And it was convincing.

Convincing enough to secure a start-up business loan for her e-commerce business where she'd combine great wine and customer service.

It's been years since then and the early days were murderous. Testing supplier problems and warehousing issues caused some pain. But that time spent researching and understanding meant that she knew how to solve them or who to seek out as accomplices.

That level of research is a luxury for most career changers, but it provided Lindsay with a real certainty and sure-footedness about her future. Now, she rarely comes across problems that she hasn't heard a version of before.

When I met Lindsay to discuss the death of her first career and the unveiling of her current career, I wondered how she compared the two very different, but very successful careers. This is what she said.

> *"Every day I know I made the right decision. I feel mainly freedom. Whilst I enjoyed working in my last organisation, I feel liberated from the bubble of that world, from the commute and from the structure.*
>
> *I'm enjoying the freedom of a new world out there. Listening to my old colleagues and others in the industry, I know the business cycle never truly changes and I feel some relief that I'm not still in that cycle. Now, I spend every day learning something totally new."*

Reversed Psychology

Joanne

Serial entrepreneur to digital development within a charity

Some professionals appear to feel so comfortable with career change, that they do it with ease, regularly. But when you scratch beneath the surface, you often discover that, while they have changed careers multiple times, the jobs they change to have very similar qualities and allow them to stay within their comfort zone. Examples include individuals who change companies often but perform similar work, or individuals who change industries but use similar skills.

Joanne was someone I had always thought of as a serial entrepreneur. When she offered to tell me the story behind her radical career change, I was intrigued.

"Class, your attention! Some of you have mastered the basics of turning frogs into chalices without too many mishaps. Today, we are advancing to human metamorphosis. I shall demonstrate. One. Two. Three. Imperomutatio! Who would like to go first?"

Joanne had always been a talented spellcaster and the youngest in her class to master the skill behind metamorphosis. A natural. She could probably have delivered lectures on human metamorphosis at the country's most prestigious schools of magic.

Over the duration of her working life, she had pointed her wand directly at herself and her career countless times.

She cast her first spell just as she completed her degree from the impressive National Ministry of Theatre Studies.

One. Two. Three. Imperomutatio!

Just like that, she had transfigured from new graduate into owner and Grand Professor of the Dark Arts of Dance and Drama at the famous school where she'd taught on a part-time basis.

Over her nine-year tenure, this talented spellcaster pointed her business wand at every tip-tapping corner of the business and doubled its size before selling it to a new talented professor from an overseas ministry.

Her next metamorphosis was initiated shortly after the birth of the new generation of magical talents in Joanne's coven. The boy with the giant smile, she named him George.

From new mother to mini-wizard party business owner.

One. Two. Three. Imperomutatio!

She worked mostly at the weekends, when her husband could be with the smiling George. The non-wizards and non-witches enjoyed the parties. She learned the whacky wizardry of community group marketing which helped the business to elevate and levitate over the next seven years.

Until... she realised something.

While she was away running the mini-wizard parties, Joanne was missing out on enchanting spells that were being cast at home. She wanted to be with her own mini wizard at the weekend. She sensed a new transfiguring spell brewing, but needed the right idea.

An advertisement in the Daily Forecaster caught her eye. They sought a qualified magician to transform the digital know-how of mothers wishing to return to work or to start their own businesses.

She would continue the mini-wizard parties and at the same time perform the digital training role and watch to see what happened. Nothing to lose.

One. Two. Three. Imperomutatio!

That digital training transformation spawned yet another opportunity to buy into a new business community franchise which would return even more of her weekends to her. A no-brainer.

Imperomutatio! Whoops.

That one didn't turn out as she expected. Perhaps her wand was on the blink and needed replacing?

While she waited for Amazon to deliver her new wand, she took a walk of reflection around the Boundless Lake.

The smiling George was preparing to step onto a new stage, his first year at secondary school. Joanne really wanted more than just weekends, she wanted family fun and exploration. She wanted to do valuable work, but she also wanted some real downtime. Non-thinking time. Nonworking time.

Bolts of inspiration swirled around in her brain. An idea crash-landed from the backyard of her memory. In between transformations, she had done some freelancing for a charity and remembered it feeling like the most satisfying magic she'd ever performed.

The idea grew wings.

A contrary idea.

The reverse of how others had done it before her. One that this successful entrepreneurial changeling hadn't expected. But the idea stuck.

One last metamorphosis.

She would seek out a *proper job*. A proper job within a charity. She would combine all her magic learned over twenty years. Then squeeze her spell making into five days of each week and lock her wand in its case at the weekend.

Regular magic-making hours. No longer the sole magic maker, working alone. Joining a team of magic makers. Sharing the magic responsibilities.

Laying down her wand in favour of family weekends. To travel. To play. To cook. To eat out. Together.

She was ready to stop negotiating time and just enjoy it. She was ready to stop transforming and to release herself from the constant pressure of creating new magic ideas every minute of every day. She was also ready to free herself from the never-endingness of entrepreneurial life.

But this metamorphosis was trickier than all her others.

Slower than the previous flicks of her magic wand. There were lots of brooms flying through the air. Invisible elements outside her control. But, after a time, her presence was requested for interview at four different Ministries of Charitable Arts.

Two progressed to final meetings with the Chief Executive Magicians. Both were gruelling. She would have loved both but had to wait for them to decide. This new game would have some frustrations.

One selected her and requested that she point her transformation skills at their digital team. To bring her magic to their learned Royal School of Horticulture and Gardening. She agreed to one last metamorphosis... perhaps.

One. Two. Three. Imperomutatio!

When I met Joanne a year or so into her new career, she was bubbling with excitement. Whilst she had felt very comfortable with career change so long as she was the business owner, she viewed her most recent reinvention as very much outside her comfort zone. Here's how she described the results from her most recent metamorphosis.

> *"For pretty much twenty years I worked on weekends. Now, I actually get that Friday feeling. I love my job **and** I love my two days of freedom at the weekend to do whatever we want. This is my first proper job. I've never had regular monthly pay and it's bloody lovely! It feels amazing!*
>
> *But the work itself is also really great. I thought that working in an organisation and not just for myself would mean that it would take longer to see results. But in the time I've been here, I feel that I've made a difference. I feel like I'm part of a team that is making a huge impact and we have big plans for the future. I feel like I'm contributing to something very exciting."*

The Sticky End of Cultural Clash

Nick

***Director within a private equity-owned business to the same
role within a private business***

Some successful professionals find themselves in a situation where they
are unable to use the skills that made them successful. If this situation
carries on for long, it becomes stressful. Long-term stress doesn't only
impact the mind. Over time, if not addressed, it starts to have a physical
impact. If ignored, our bodies will continue to send us warning messages
until we listen and act.

Nick was someone who had blocked out his whispered warning
messages for so long that the messages had begun to shout very loudly
indeed. He needed a very serious incident to fully realise that ignoring
stress was a dangerous game to play.

Until recently, Lady Luck had been on his side. Yet, she was a fickle muse, capricious in whim and loyalty.

As far as work was concerned, Nick felt like he'd hit the jackpot. Work felt like a game that he loved and it loved him back. One he excelled at, bet wisely and sauntered home satisfied with his monthly winnings.

The financial stakes were always high, but the personal stakes were not outrageous. Everyone bought in, worked hard and won often. A challenging poker game rather than a high-stakes, high-rolling, risk-it-all craps game.

With Lady Luck always beside him, he had never experienced the darker side of the game until the casino changed hands.

The new private equity owners arrived one day. They changed the stakes, the tables and ultimately the game. Their veneer of pleasantry disappeared within weeks to unveil gangster requests for human investment. Relentless demands for power. Trust had disappeared and everyone felt that the house was betting against them. Even Lady Luck struggled to hide her displeasure.

The new mob had no need for his talents. A top-of-his-game poker player was transformed into an exhausted slot machine, spewing data for who knows what purpose.

He felt Lady Luck squeeze his hand gently, telling him to be careful. But he was powerless against their Godfatherly orders. The longer he played, the more the odds stacked against him and the more Lady Luck chastised him.

Over time their demands began to erode him to the core. Chipping away at his life force. Questioning his need to be there. He had bought into the game and felt trapped. And wearing his poker face, pretending he didn't care, was stressful. He felt exhausted from late-night games with no purpose.

Click.

Swallow.

Pop.

Nick's new daily pill-popping routine, more suited to an 87-year-old than a 47-year-old. When the chips were down, he agreed it wasn't working. But didn't know how to exit without bloodshed. So, he just kept medicating the stress away.

Beyond head and heart, there were other signs that things weren't going so well.

Sighing had become part of his hourly routine. His early morning chats with colleagues before work had been silenced. A new exercise regime consisted of collapsing on the bed every evening and an anxiety-filled sleep. Annual invitations to family and friends' celebrations were declined. Two years in a row.

Worrying looks grew into worried words from his caring wife. Thankfully the child appeared not to notice... the absence.

The absence of his joyful, chilled beer in the garden. The absence of light at his home times. The absence of attendances at violin recitals and parents' evenings. The absence of carefree cuddles. The absence of genuine interest—in anything.

A grand theft had occurred. The theft of his happiness.

This sleight of hand was deathly slow and barely recognisable in the mirror. Others had noticed it first. That his sparkle had disappeared. His sense of humour had aged. His shoulders rounded to protect himself. Extra weight gained as armour to shield him from more futile dice rolling and their just-do-it culture.

Pride and the lack of a good Plan B meant he'd stick and play safe rather than exit the game.

But safe wasn't truly safe, was it?

A career coach, an old contact, came on the scene and helped him uncover his superpowers. She tried to figure out what was stopping him from releasing himself from this nightmare. She worried openly and thought she'd failed.

But he was a strong one and needed *even* more real evidence to cash in his chips.

Lady Luck had decided enough was enough and stood to announce her departure. As she deserted Nick, she screamed and then touched his heart just once. Her final hint should he wish to listen.

The doctor then dealt him his last chance card. It said, *Stop or be stopped.*

45

Tipping point reached. He cashed in his chips to negotiate an exit. He exited the casino and gave up gambling with his life.

Many months of recovery. More months of rebuilding and replenishing what had been lost. He sought evidence that there was another way. He realised he hadn't hated his job. He'd hated the culture. The culture that had punched him in the heart.

Rebuild complete. An old contact and trusted friend invited him to join a completely different game. A small one where the stakes were lower, where he could design the rules.

His way. With his flair. And his talents. Getting his hands dirtier than they'd been in a while. He would deal the cards. The tables would not be rigged against him. There would be no requirement for endless late-night games. A boss with matched values.

Nick left behind the game of chance and chose a game of skill instead.

When I met Nick, he reflected on how it could have been different had he not taken control when he had enough energy to rebuild himself and ready himself for a different kind of work.

"Looking back with the benefit of hindsight, I genuinely believe I was close to going under or worse. My mind and body were compromised and at the edge of their tolerance levels. A serious health scare provided the catalyst for me to leave, but I still needed the willpower and strength to make that final decision. I'm very glad that I jumped while I had the strength!

My bounce is back and I am genuinely excited by what lies ahead."

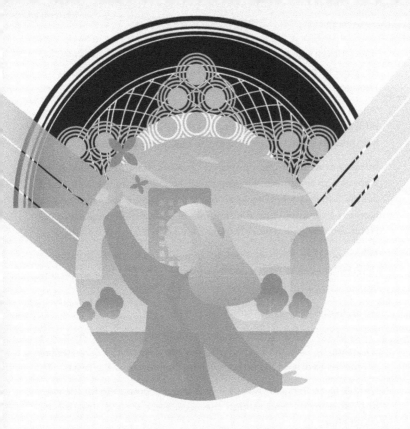

Ignored Instincts

Karen

Head Teacher to food entrepreneur

We get so used to thinking our careers are linear and many of us can empathise with Karen's decision. Go to the top of her profession or stay at a level, in a role that she thoroughly enjoyed? Sadly, she didn't listen to her instincts when she was offered a head teacher role. This is what happened.

Fireworks crackled inside her pleasure sensors as she negotiated her way through a variety of inner-city schools and schools in deprived areas. Karen had known from the first day of her teacher training course that she had found her place in the world. Even on the tough days, she felt needed and wanted by parents, her fellow teachers and not least by the children. She felt in her bones that this was to be her life's work and she could never stop learning how to improve.

When a door to a school for young people with complex learning difficulties opened, her curiosity and desire to keep learning escorted her through its arches, onto new and rewarding challenges.

Success and satisfaction powered up more fizzing fireworks in the form of a promotion to Deputy Head Teacher. Karen thrived doing deeply fulfilling teaching work alongside training new teachers to increase their impact on the children. She flourished supporting the Head Teacher, doing work that mattered and using her talents.

When another door opened to a head teacher's position in a different specialist school, she hesitated for the first time in her life. Not knowing why.

Something wasn't quite right.

A sea of flattery drowned out her instincts. All she could hear was a barrage of "You are perfect. It's your ideal next move." So she felt compelled to attend the interview. It hushed the crowd at least.

Unable to do things by halves, it was stressful preparing for the two-day assessment, even though she never once thought they would choose her.

But choose her they did. She felt flattered again but wasn't at all sure she could do it... even if she wanted to.

If they thought she could do it, maybe she could?

But the turmoil began brewing in the deep pit of her stomach. Darkening and shadowing her from within. Gathering her nagging doubts one by one and meticulously smothering them in a black bag of it'll-be-oks. Methodically gagging every niggling worry in case they escaped into her real world and spoiled it... for everyone. Gradually, the silence prevailed.

Inhale. She grabbed the darkness-filled black bag. Squished it into its storage-box prison. Slammed the lid shut. And shoved it in a wardrobe at the back of her attic. In a spot it would never be discovered. Exhale.

Then she accepted the role.

How could she have known it would go so wrong?

But the children needed help and she knew how to help them. The responsibility heaved itself up on her narrow shoulders. Burdening her evenings and her weekends.

With every stressful occurrence, of which there were many, those slight shoulders grew heavier and heavier. Diminishing her blow by blow.

Never-ending housework. School work never done. Children could be helped if she had the right support. But difficulties mounted issue by issue. Harder work. Bigger problems. Until her shoulder bones almost fractured.

Her husband worried greatly for her health. Others did too. But onwards and downwards she persisted. Almost breaking and always bruising from the inside out. On the day a giant crack appeared, she agreed to resign.

There was little left of her to offer.

She crawled into bed in her attic room to unpack that box filled with the worries. As she liberated her doubts and worries into the light, she realised they needed her to listen. At that point, she began to recover.

Her lovely, supportive husband, Julian, brought coffee filled with cuddles. Talking, sharing, supporting. Pushing the colour back into her, cuppa by cuppa. Rebuilding her little by little.

Slowly and unsurely, she recuperated, regaining her trust in herself. And six weeks later she emerged, like a flower from the attic, less bashed and bruised but still shaken.

They had talked for years about a passion for good food with flavour. They wondered if now was the moment? If by working together, she would thrive once again, caring about a business together?

She agreed she was ready. And so was he. They would create their long-held dream. Nothing fancy and Nowt Poncy, they crafted their new brand of delicious, healthy sauces together.

Working in a role that does not utilise your superpowers is uncomfortable, at best, but can be debilitating over time. Sometimes a role change or a promotion feels very stressful for this reason. When I asked Karen how she was enjoying using her superpowers to create her new career alongside someone she trusts and loves, this was her response.

"It feels incredible to be working on our business with Julian all day. We have such a great partnership. I couldn't do this without him—I have so much appreciation for his talents and his driving force."

Non, Je Ne Regrette Rien!

Julian

Own business to corporate role to food entrepreneur

Some career changers hold the seed of a new career dream for a long time, sometimes for years or even decades, waiting and hoping for the right moment to release it into the world. Fear of failure is often tied up with this sort of delayed career change. But if the dream is to become a reality, at some point the fear of not trying must outweigh the fear of potential failure.

This becomes an *I know I'll regret it if I don't do it* moment which can be nurtured into a very strong motivating force towards action. This was the case for Julian and his wife Karen (from the previous story) who

After Karen's recovery from her very stressful step down from her head teacher's role, Julian and she discussed whether this was their now-or-never opportunity. They had always talked about their mutual passion for healthy, home-cooked food and wondered if they could actually produce a simple sauce that the market would like.

I took her jewelled hand in my hand again,

as we imagined our lives ending without giving it a try.

Our under the covers, one day, whispered dream.

She nodded and smiled her encouraging smile

and said, "If not now, then when?"

We clutched our dream, our first recipe, close to our hearts.

Sped back to university, to scientists we trusted

to taste it, then tell us we were crazy.

We're not, it appears. Then they pointed us in next-step directions

to craft this tasty dream into a jarred reality.

After tasting their sauces, a local butcher offered to sell some of their home-made tomato and basil sauce and the locals loved it. They then took their first sauce back to their old university and the food scientists, who loved it and gave them lots of advice on where to start learning what they needed to learn as a new entrant into the complex food industry.

Our own little food company, where we would endeavour

to rid the world of nasties-packed sauces,

one tempting taste bud at a time.

We created sauces from scratch and for health

for busy parents with no time to stew.

Oh, the dream appeared simple, a line drawing or two

The reality, an encyclopaedia of learning.

So much to do, so little time.

A sardine in a shark tank of major food corporations

as they readied to swallow us whole.

The journey from zero to producing one jar for sale to the general public was a journey that neither had anticipated. They needed to learn about labelling, bottling, food hygiene, food testing, trademarks, branding, design and legal requirements. Even as a new entrant in the industry, they had to adhere to the same standards as the major food companies. Sometimes they felt that the task was beyond them but when they received fantastic comments from first-time tasters, their resolve strengthened.

But little means slippery with freedom to experiment.

Bigger is slower and less nimble

All things come to those who swim fast.

We believed, had courage and knew they'd want it

A generation craving speed-food that needn't be ghastly

Today, I'm in pieces, I'm feeling totally wrung out

The hours, travel and the constant learning.

Even if we were in our thirties, we'd still be exhausted.

But we're in our fifties, it's tricky keeping up

but we're doing what we love and it feels fantastic!

Both Julian and Karen in our conversations emphasised how they wished they had started their business much earlier, thinking that being younger with more energy might have helped them. At the same time, they also felt grateful for the life experience those extra twenty years afforded them. In the end they said that it all evens out.

So, we breathe a sigh of relief.

It's very possible, if we keep learning enough.

Keep kicking faster every minute of the day

to stay afloat as we grow to compete

And when we're old, we'll sing Hallelujah… No regrets!

Julian and his wife Karen were motivated to live a life with no regrets and decided to create their dream at their now-or-never moment. Their tenacity and desire to learn has allowed them to gain real traction as a new market entrant in a tough industry. I wondered how it felt for Julian to be living his long-held dream. This is what he said.

"We have definitely done the right thing! Every day, we wake up to our new selves. We are loving creating and growing the Nowt Poncy brand, one mouth at a time.

It feels so fantastic when we watch people taste our products for the first time. Their eyes sort of pop open with the 'My God, it tastes home-made!' feeling."

The Wondering Years

David

Full-time accounting specialist to flexible contracting.

The most common response to my question about how it feels to have changed career, revolves around the theme of freedom. Freedom to choose work style, content, timing and environment. Sometimes, that very adult sense of freedom and choice gets lost within major corporations. When it does, it can drive us to rebel and to want to write a different story. When I met David, he had one very particular style of story on his mind.

Once upon a time, there lived a most remarkable boy called David who had been given a special gift. In all the land, there had never been anybody like David. He could read the stories that numbers told.

. day growing up, from little clogs to big, he would practise his magic abilities in the kitchen parlour until the day he was ready to leave his village to take his gift to university and beyond.

He packed his bags and began his quest at the grand halls of KPMG with lots of other number-gifted children from far-off lands. He'd enrolled in the grandest of the grand number-story-telling guilds.

In the beginning he loved it. There was so much to learn. Such great friendships and challenging quests, more numerous than dragons at a gathering of fair maidens.

But some years later, a realisation dawned that would put an end to his endeavours at those grand halls. He discovered that he was different from the others.

They possessed an ambition-fuelled hunger to be knighted as partners. A hunger he had never felt. A hunger he knew he would never, ever feel.

Bidding farewell to the future partners, David set off in search of a true and fair king. A king with a wish to grow his kingdom. A king who would appreciate his gift

At the same time, he began to craft the most perfect happily ever after story. He and his wife had created a wonderful family with three little additions who multiplied his life's richness beyond his number stories.

It was no coincidence that he chose to work just five miles away from his village. He could use his gift by day and ride home by night to read bedtime stories and kiss foreheads goodnight. But it was not to be.

His work was an insatiable monster with a ravenous appetite for number stories. Wicked demands for his night-times, his energy and more than a little of his heart.

The monster's unquenchable desire for endless tales had consumed many a merry band of number-story-tellers. But, new unknowing, guileless tale-tellers always arrived at the gates to the castle eager to practise their gifts.

Until one day, after feeding the monster from dawn to dusk, he slumped in his ergonomically designed throne. And gazed from the window of his brightly lit, soulless, gleaming, glassed castle. Beyond the multitude of soulless, gleaming, glassed castles, each with their own hungry monsters, he could just make out his village.

He wondered how his little 'un, the youngest of the three, was enjoying his bedtime story. How his first day at little knight school had gone. How tired and lonely his wife felt after feeding, bathing and putting the wee ones to bed alone, after a long day of toiling over the kitchen fire.

It was torture not being there but what could he do?

He was torn.

He wanted and needed to put his talent to good use. But he also wanted to be there to read bedtime stories to his offspring. Important learning stories that children might remember... forever. Tales of freedom, adventure and endeavour for good causes.

Just a few miles stood between him and those bedtime stories, but he might as well have been in another kingdom, on another world.

Must he be chained to the desk so late at night? It's hard to see stories in numbers in the middle of the night.

Requesting the monster's permission to take leave from the castle to attend school jousts and inter-kingdom tournaments or to read bedtime stories had begun to gnaw away at his core.

He would just escape. Should.

But he could not escape.

His fatherly responsibilities. His family to feed and clothe. His promised pot of gold at the end of a rainbow-coloured, long-term incentive plan. If he could just remain chained to the desk for a few more years, the golden egg of freedom would be his.

But he could not remain.

Powerless against his monster eating his magic moments of family time. Cursed to remain in the monster's castle for what felt like an eternity.

Something within David died that night.

But in that one death, a new possibility was born.

David requested an opinion from his fairy godmother HR Director. Her advice, like a wave of a magic wand, transformed everything.

She suggested that rather than riding in a pumpkin, the carriage of a contractor might offer him a lifestyle with the freedom he wished for. The idea sparkled immediately. He knew what to do.

As soon as the town crier announced his decision, a maternity-leave contract magically appeared.

He grasped it with both hands. One contract led to another. Over time he carved out a name for himself as a contractor who could solve a very specific style of story-telling problem with his special gift.

He would receive a decent bag of coins for a decent day's toil. As time wore on, he freed himself from the monster's ravenous appetites and its rainbow-coloured, long-term incentive plans.

At the same time, he and his wife enjoyed watching the wee ones grow up. Enjoying his work and reading bedtime stories from comfy chairs in their cosy castle. Revelling in his freedom. Delighting in the fairer balance between work and family. Not missing the shackles of the gleaming, glassed castle and its endless desire for more of him and his.

But one day, when his pumpkin-riding scars had almost healed, a charming but selfish prince tapped him on the shoulder to entice him back. David's talents were tantalised by the magnificent problem needing to be solved and he agreed to a secret meeting.

All went well. For the first few moments.

Then he spied the annual holiday scroll hidden from view. A feather pen had inked out the entire month of August. His throat constricted. Claustrophobia set in.

He distracted the selfish prince with a looking glass and fled.

Was the contractor's carriage the perfect fit for this talented young boy, all grown up? Of course not. Perfect only exists in fairy tales.

Prices and demand for his talents in the towns and villages nearby often fluctuated beyond his control. Some days his bag of magic beans was smaller than he hoped. Other days it was larger.

But as time went by, David's beans grew into strong stalks through recommendations and honourable mentions. He felt valuable and valued doing good work. His dream of spending six summer weeks having fun with those wee ones was no longer just a fantasy.

He believed in his ability to use his talents in a way that worked for the monsters, the individual and the family at the same time.

David's children are older now. Their needs rarely involve bedtime stories any more. He still rides the carriage of a contractor and has carved it in a way that he can be with his teenage almost-knights for their summer—even if they sometimes ignore him.

Whilst David's story is far from ended, there have been many glimpses of a life lived happily... perhaps ever after.

When David and I met, he remained absolutely certain that leaving behind the permanent pumpkin and riding in his contractor's carriage was the right thing for both himself and his family. He boiled the essence of his career satisfaction down to just one thing.

"Freedom is important to me. The shackles and small print of long-term incentive programmes don't work for me. I want to get paid for doing good work—it's that simple."

Are You There, God?
It's Me, Creativity

Clare

Mother to mother, illustrator, author and fashion influencer

Other career changers set off without a very clear or specific idea where they are headed, but with a desire to use their skills and talents and see where they might lead. They let the end goals evolve depending on how and where their skills and talents land best.

In the meantime, they use the skills that they love using, that make them feel great. Then they begin to figure out how to commercialise those skills. It can seem counter-intuitive to some, but the idea has gained

Alone at the kitchen table, husband still at work, baby girl finally asleep, Clare rolled a pencil in her fingers. Over and over. Pondering quietly.

She was reconnecting with an old friend, excited but worried. Questioning whether her talent would return to her. Whether age and years apart would have affected the relationship between fingers, brain and heart.

She questioned whether resuscitating the skill could fill the empty hole that had somehow appeared. Created in the space between wifeville, motherland, sisterhood and daughtertown.

The space between all that she was and might be.

She remembered the moment she'd been slapped in the face. By the promise of an idea.

It had been a long time coming. It had travelled 14,000 miles. When she had unwrapped it from its ribboned packaging, it peeped out to reveal an idea for her future.

It was a book, neither plain nor simple. A book to behold. A book for a little girl who loved fashion. It was a book to inspire her to draw again.

She had been drifting for a while. After her degree in illustration, she had worked in retail, met a gorgeous man and fallen in love. They married and then relocated back to his homeland.

That night, she opened her specially bought sketching paper. Released her pencils from an old box in the attic. Inhaling the leaded perfume, Claire relived moments of great joy and deep fulfilment.

The second the pencil touched the paper, it all came flooding back.

She felt connection in every stroke. The pencil began to fill in her empty space.

As she sketched, the eyes and face of a little girl were revealed. The little girl that sleeping baby might become.

She added dresses and shoes. Dressing up with her mummy. Little feet in mummy's gorgeous shoes. Hearts and eyes lifted. Sharing the dressing up fun together. Special colour-filled moments.

A moment of creation. Something. Something just hers. It was there all the time. Just sitting at her kitchen table.

Now started, she couldn't stop. She sketched every night. She refined and recreated. Started over and over again. Until she had completed her first creation.

A children's book, with her love of fashion and style embedded.

A calm little story for mummies like her. Who loved children but didn't erase all that they were before. She was ready to release it.

Now off to find a publisher, surely not too hard? Endless weeks later, she was to be proven wrong.

Down but not out, she decided to self-publish. All new learning. All new risks. She took her savings and folded them up in her book, determined to get it printed. The books arrived off a boat, in a big box, front covers on backwards, egg noodles between pages where savings had been.

More savings to find a new printer, a better choice this time. Then off to promote it.

Book fair after book fair, she sold nothing but kept plugging away with her belief and her head held high.

She kept battling on, sometimes daunted and deflated. Persisting knowing one day it would click. The click happened when a call came from an editor who had met her on a zero-sales day. Asked to feature her in an article. Excitedly, she agreed and over time that meeting turned into a regular column in that national magazine.

She had lifted off and it felt great. She wanted more so pushed on with new ideas and more book sales. She was discovered by new people and asked to do more, things that she'd never imagined.

Personalised illustrated commissions, brand ambassador work, asked to wear designer dresses to major functions and her own brand of stationery. And that little book of shoes turned into another on bags with a third in the design stage. Lots of new unimagined experiences.

Clare has three children now and could never have imagined what meeting the right people at the right time could have done for her. When we caught up, I asked her how it feels to have created her new career doing things that she absolutely loves. This was her response.

"When I get those emails or comments from mums who have read my book to their children, and they choose their favourite pages—it's a fantastic feeling. I feel very fortunate to be able to do what I love and work with such inspiring people while still being a mum to my children, who are my main priority.

As I look back, I realise that every time I thought I was being rejected from something good, I was actually being redirected to something better."

Colouring in When the Wolves Are at the Door

Charlotte

**_Corporate Social Media Manager to
PR business for food business owners_**

When career changers are considering setting up their first business, timing is crucial. Often a now-or-never moment either appears or is created. That moment provides the necessary impetus to take that first, sometimes difficult, step.

That now-or-never feeling was very prominent in Charlotte's story. It prompted her to make the decision to step away from the comfort zone of a role that she no longer enjoyed, to jump into the exciting unknown. It was not all a bed of roses though.

Charlotte's fingers, toes and eyelashes had been crossed in hope for so long they resembled an archaic ruin matted with the tangled remains of withered ivy. Hope that her name was on the redundancy list. Hope that she could be freed from the mangled roots of her corporate life.

And released from the boredom. Hacked free from the roots before they completely encased her within their evermore.

It was hard to imagine how it had come to this in a few short-long years.

She had thrived as the founding member of the inaugural social media team, planted within one of the biggest supermarkets in the country. She had blossomed within the culture of creative possibilities, helping an already huge brand to flourish, supported by enormous budgets. She adored hanging out at Facebook and Twitter headquarters to learn from the best. Creating and blooming in perfect harmony.

Then a change in strategy was announced. All the clever, interesting work was outsourced to creative agencies and the in-house work became dull.

Almost overnight her blossom withered.

Culling rather than creating. Editing rather than designing. Adhering to corporate guidelines. The colour had drained from her work and began to drain from her stem. Choking the vibrance from her soul.

Three times she read the names on the list. Slowly, just in case she'd missed it. She hadn't. It wasn't there.

Resigned disbelief. She had had a feeling. They wanted her to remain as the squashed social media marketing gardener.

Head and heart drooped. What now? The buds of excitement could not be ungrown. Corporate life had already been pruned from her life and her mind. She couldn't stay stuck.

With resigned disbelief her head and heart handed in their notice. To explore new pastures in which to replant those creative buds.

In recent years, Charlotte has spent blissful, colourful weekends at food festivals, farmers markets and independent food shows. A northern lass chattering, buzzing with energy amongst a glorious meadow of food lovers. Tasting, testing, smelling, questioning, laughing and sharing stories. These were her people. Her clan.

A germ of an idea sprouted. She could use her copywriting talents to help her clan grow just as she had helped her previous business grow. Imagine the giant spurts she could engineer if she adored the products and the people behind those products.

A completely different work proposition. One that would nourish and sustain her. One that would allow her to blossom once more. She loved the idea so much that she would almost do it for free.

After allowing the idea to germinate, she launched her copywriting business and began to sow seeds of her offering with all her foodie clan, believing it to be a no-brainer.

A year later, she opened the bank statement she'd avoided for too long. Knowing it signalled the death knell of her beautiful business.

Twelve months of tending, nurturing and loving every moment hadn't been enough.

Her hemlock bank balance screamed at her "GET A JOB!" She struggled to imagine leaving behind her stunning creation to wither and die.

At rock bottom, her desire to continue working with her band of foodies could not be felled. Backed into a shaded, tear-dampened corner beside a giant love-lies-bleeding plant, her creative mind chanced upon the nub of the problem.

Her tribe, the food business owners, had no clue what copywriting was or why it should be a priority. All they wanted was a little more publicity to help their businesses blossom in the same way that they, as individuals, were blossoming doing work that they loved.

Overnight, with the help of her loving partner she cleared her business allotment. Replanted, rebranded and renamed it. They created a new website and developed her new PR company helping business owners to do their own publicity in ten minutes a day.

She tended to the shoots of these young food businesses. She offered them PR nourishment to allow them to flourish through publicity. Article by article, magazine by magazine, mention by mention.

The sun began to truly shine on Charlotte's business second time around and boy did it flower! Several years later, the shoots of success have flourished into rather large blooms. She's now experiencing success to complement her love of doing business with her passionate clan.

Charlotte's story of tenacity in the face of possible business failure really inspired me. When I had the opportunity to talk to her partner David, a designer, I asked him if he had noticed any changes in her since she left the corporate world behind. His response just blew me away.

"Charlotte's nine-to-five corporate role turned her into a monotone grey, but when she broke the chains and started doing something she truly loved, she erupted into a rainbow of colour."

And here's what Charlotte said.

"I can't believe I get to do this as a job! I'm excited to get out of bed in the morning. I work with my ideal clients who are passionate about their food like me. I don't think I could get this level of satisfaction from working in a corporate."

Whose Path Is This Anyway?

Anil

Global corporate career to start-up

It's not so common but some career changers know exactly where they want to end up but haven't figured out how to get there yet. They don't let that get in the way. By actively building their skills, attitudes and experiences, the path becomes clearer along the way. They have faith that it will happen but take actions to make sure that they are ready when opportunity comes knocking. Anil is one of these individuals.

Anil hadn't just climbed his career ladder. He'd sprinted up every ladder that was ever placed in front of him and then hurdled onto the next.

Economics degree. Summer internships. Investment banking. MBA from Wharton. McKinsey. Fortune 500. FTSE 100. London, New York, Paris, Geneva, Stockholm.

He had changed teams often, but this conditioned athlete raced like a champion, no matter which team he raced for. A sure bet, his eyes were set on his next goal. Fixed directly towards a country leadership role, the next rung on his global corporate career ladder.

But a niggling feeling had begun to jiggle this particular ladder, more and more often. Eyes on the prize, true to form, he tried to ignore the distraction and charged ever forwards.

His impending fortieth birthday had momentarily distracted his focus from that country leadership race, allowing him to pause his training to step back and assess the bigger picture, not just the next goal in a successful career. He paused long enough to question if he even cared for the prize at the end of this race.

In truth, Anil had been feeling like a little cog in a big wheel for a while now. His rebellious actions had gone unnoticed by his coaches. He had disguised them as tiny little side projects.

Like those extra university courses in chemistry and biology or that Chartered Financial Analyst qualification, both gained in his rest time. None of these extras sat on the right track or field. They certainly were not on his training plan.

But they fuelled Anil's insatiable hunger to learn more about things that mattered to him. He filled his spare brain space with skills and knowledge, sort of knowing he might use them some day.

Although he had performed well in all sorts of international championships, Anil was unsatisfied with his performance. He needed to use more talents and skills, more often. To do more and learn more in every day.

In short, he knew he had more to offer but wasn't sure where to offer it or to whom.

So, he decided to offer more to his Regional MD. Not the done thing. But he persisted. He offered his MD a piece of market analysis that would allow Anil to use more of his skills. He offered it with zero expectations.

Impressed, six months later, that same MD offered him a gift in return. A new role to start up a small business within their big business. A seasoned athlete by now, Anil vaulted into this new world, into a race that would change his future.

The next two years were the best years in his career, he'd found his Olympic circuit. He loved racing on that shorter race track. He felt faster and infinitely more crucial. There were fewer mammoth strategies and more day-to-day influence, where of all his decisions mattered. Where his tiny new team were in charge of the successes and, of course, the failures.

He had found his new race, on a completely different track on a completely different field. One that he'd consciously chosen this time. He knew his future lay in start-ups or early-stage businesses. He wanted to hold success and failure in his hands every day, not to watch from a lofty box above the stands.

New race agreed.

He now needed a new training plan.

He started with research on young companies, cultures, attitudes and expectations so that he could understand what they expected. One sticking point confirmed a major difference he had already guessed. That salaries were much lower. But potential winnings much higher. Sure bets don't exist in start-ups, so they want their teams to share the risk.

It all made sense until Anil discovered he was trapped. Trapped by his wonderful lifestyle.

He discussed the upsides and the downsides with his wife and children. If Anil wanted to do this very exciting and hopefully happier work, they would need to live differently to allow it. The gorgeous big apartment was exchanged for a smaller home. Then they freed themselves from the unnecessary spending that would keep their daddy and husband trapped climbing someone else's ladder and performing in his old race team forever.

Then to the search for the ideal new track and to figure out which might best use his skills. After applying for lots of advertised positions, one appeared especially perfect.

He wanted them.

And thankfully they wanted him.

This new track was far from a breeze. But the thrills of that race meant that he learned much more in a short time than he had for years on the other tracks. It had changed him. After eighteen months his first race was over, as is common with young businesses. Owners and investors changed teams more regularly than big corporations. Their races are sprints not marathons.

But this sprint confirmed to Anil that he had chosen the right sort of race. His experience on this new track had opened so many more career opportunities in different arenas that Anil is now spoilt for choice for his next race.

When I interviewed Anil about his very conscious planning to get to his chosen race course, he emphasised the role that downsizing his financial outgoings had played in putting him and his family in the right position to take the exciting opportunity when it arose. I was curious how he enjoyed the reality behind smaller business dynamics. This is what he said.

"With this start-up experience under my belt, my whole future career options have been multiplied. I've got so many more options than I had with my career history two years ago. Putting your career on autopilot doesn't serve anyone well.

Just because you are on a path doesn't mean it is the right path. I feel so lucky. I love being a part of companies where every big decision is made by a handful of people and working in an industry that excites me."

Premeditated Inventions with Baked Beans

Ges

Lifetime banker to public speaking trainer

If you worked hard to be successful in one career, there is absolutely no reason why you couldn't be successful in a different career. But choosing your next career, one that you could do forever, can take time and often a little guidance. When I met Ges, he told me his inspirational story of discovering his final career in his fifties with a fair few bumps along the way.

Thunk! Thunk! He soundchecked the microphone, after jaunting up the stairs while the audience hushed in anticipation. He took a barely noticeable deep breath of bravery and launched himself into the sheen of the spotlight to begin his set.

"Did you hear the one about the friendly bank manager?"

"He was redundant."

Ges exited his first career with an unexpected lightness of foot and humour.

A whole swathe of the leadership team had been ushered into bleak meeting rooms and escorted out again with mechanical swiftness. After twenty-five years in the bank, from chief tea-makers to managers, an entire generation of bankers had been offered the chance to stick around for heart attacks and early graves.

Alternatively, they could disappear peacefully with a juicy cheque in their top pockets.

The majority signed the papers before they had even landed on the table.

With cash in the bank, Ges stepped into a new rollercoaster world of SMEs. S for small amounts of cash, M for medium amounts of longevity and E for exciting opportunities for energy depletion.

A decade later, although the highs and lows had excited him, they had exhausted his personal bank manager's sense of humour. He'd experienced lots of different roles within dynamic, early-stage, high-growth businesses. As it also turned out, overly ambitious, mightily stretched and cash-strapped businesses.

Three redundancies later, with minimal or non-existent severance packages, his bank account had been drained.

Through no fault of his own, his small business career nosedived and crashed, smashing him straight through the front door of the local unemployment office.

At an all-time low, the benefits queue sharpened his mind to figure out the next move. This time he needed help from new partners.

Serendipity, happenstance and wisdom.

Happenstance came in the form of both his daughters' departures for university—his household bills plummeted.

Serendipity arrived in the form of the launch of the low-cost supermarket Lidl in his town. With some careful planning and creativity with baked beans, they could afford to live on his wife's part-time salary for a time while he tried something new.

Wisdom made itself known in Ges' cluelessness. Having accepted that he was stuck and had no idea where to start, he requested the wisdom of a renowned, local career coach. He prompted Ges to rethink his past work from different angles. After dedicating more time, effort and thought than ever before to his career, he was rewarded with several light-bulb moments along the way.

Whilst swirling around in the deep dark depths of his working career and life, Ges uncovered a set of skills that he'd been polishing for most of his adult life.

Skills that others always complimented him on.

Skills that he loved using.

Skills that didn't drain the life out of him even when he used them all day. In fact, he believed he could use these skills all day, every day and never tire.

Public speaking.

It had been in his bones since the age of nineteen, when the bank had sent him on a Toastmasters course. Over the decades, he had always been called upon to make speeches, present awards and MC events. And he had happily volunteered his skills.

He had led courses at the bank and for a whole range of smaller businesses. He had honed these skills for thirty years. And it was only now, trying to answer the questions he had never been asked, that he realised that not everyone enjoyed public speaking the way he did.

When he considered it, most people he met actually *hated* public speaking. But didn't most senior jobs require it?

Perhaps?

Perhaps this could be his new business?

And so Ges began to craft his potential new career. To prepare to launch himself onto a new stage. To start a career with longevity. A career within his control.

Work he would jump out of bed to do in the morning.

Work that could sustain him for years and decades to come.

Work that he could evolve in different ways, depending on the market, which opportunities presented themselves and how he felt.

Work that he might never retire from. Ever.

He developed the idea into a business. Slowly pointing all of his natural skills at something he loved. Something that he could do better than many. And getting paid well for it.

Ges now takes his charming, light-footed, public speaking training show on the road. He steps on and off stages so regularly and so successfully that he and his wife never need to worry about living on baked beans again.

"My time is up, here. You've been a great audience. See you next time!"

Many years on, Ges spends his days helping those of us who don't love public speaking to love it more. Helping us to add a little pizazz to our public performances. His public speaking training business is going from strength to strength and he has just released his first book. When I met with the force that is Ges, I was curious to hear how he felt about his final career move. This is how he described it.

"It's absolutely liberating! I'm retirement age but the sky is my limit. Every day when I wake up, I feel like I will never be done learning. I feel respected for what I contribute and what I deliver. Not my grade. Not my job title or my years of service.

Also, the reward of building someone's confidence in public speaking and watching them spread their wings and fly is beyond any salary package."

The Exceedingly Long Haul
to Freedom

Duncan

Senior finance executive to owner of a distribution business

Some career changers feel that they are fighting against cultural shifts, philosophy swings or ownership changes that clash with their deep sense of what is important. Duncan's experience reflects this conflict. When we met, he described his reactions to changes in a business culture he didn't believe in, his extreme efforts to change that business culture and his search for the right moments to retreat and relaunch.

As he prepared to attack yet another work week, Duncan's energy reserves waned. Their depletion hadn't advanced under the cover of a single night of combat.

Instead, it was as though a brick wall had thumped itself against the same spot on the centre of his forehead again and again.

Again and again.

For almost a decade.

The resulting battle wound, almost invisible to the naked eye, disguised just enough internal damage to cause everlasting impairment.

Duncan had thoroughly enjoyed the first half of his career. He'd chosen to specialise in the most commercial, forward-looking regiment of the giant world of finance. And he'd chosen well.

The work excited him. It came naturally. He shone with purpose.

It made deep sense to him to use historical information to drive future actions, goals and strategies. Creating detailed, long-term business plans made him feel worthwhile and valuable. These plans offered a strategy to give companies the greatest chance of success. To help them move beyond defence and survival modes.

To thrive. To build the right teams. To do the right things. At the right time.

But something had changed.

The long-term focus didn't seem to matter any more. To anyone.

Except him.

Every business and every boss he'd worked for during the last ten years had become less and less concerned with success beyond the next few years. They themselves knew that they wouldn't be around beyond that time frame. They would be disappeared at the whim of shareholders, just like the last guy. There would be another guy in his place the very next morning.

The future didn't matter as much to them as it had in the past.

There was no appetite to win long-fought wars against competitors. Just the battle of the day, on the field directly in front of them.

Short-termitis had hit like a plague.

Organisational wounds were patched up and disguised with immaculate dressings for external presentation, then disregarded.

But beneath those dressings, the wounds continued to fester.

Devoting time, skills and manpower to gouge out the decaying, putrefying mess that lay beneath, offered zero short-term benefits. The long-term consequences would be the next guy's problem.

Myopic dysfunctions. Bare-knuckle boardroom brawls fought quickly with triumphant victors. This was the order of the day.

But Duncan knew that the genuine victories were to be found beyond the immediate horizon. He felt it in his wearying bones.

Try as he might, he couldn't stop banging his war drum to muster new forces.

A lone soldier waging a war against decisions that didn't make sense beyond this year.

He encouraged. He enticed. He debated.

He coaxed. He cajoled. He defended.

But the war took its toll. Sapped and battleworn, he persevered, incapable of swapping his deep-felt allegiances.

For years. And years.

Finally, seeing no way to win the war within big companies, and for the sake of his own sanity, he pointed his personal target in a completely different direction—at smaller companies.

The dream of freedom lodged in his brain.

If he were to own a small company himself, he could prove the benefits of investing in the long term *while* doing more valuable, less draining work.

But, of course, the investment capital would take time to accumulate. He relocated from the city and tightened his belt. Made tiny tactical changes while the daily grind marched onward.

Over time, savings grew while Duncan evaluated many business opportunities. But none possessed the crucial long-term potential.

Somehow the little light at the end of his dark tunnel shone just enough hope to sustain his dream of freedom.

Until the day.

The day a business presented itself. There was something very different about this business. He recognised it almost immediately.

The numbers were good, sure. But critically, the business had enduring potential and everyone working within it seemed to recognise it.

In fact, their livelihoods depended on it.

Still battle-weary, he met with the retiring owner and visited the business. It would take time, but Duncan could already feel the potential new alliance stoking the embers of his energy reserves and reinvigorating his drive.

He would be the new owner.

He packed away his drum and retreated from the ten-year war to join new forces, his new team. Side by side, they strode forward with nothing but longevity on their minds.

All willing the business to sustain them, their families and their customers far into their futures.

When I spoke to Duncan, six months after he had become the new owner, his voice had a lightness to it that I had not remembered over our years of knowing each other. I asked him about the reality behind living his dream and this is how he articulated his feelings.

"It feels easy... but scary because now I hold in my hands the mortgages of ten employees—not just my own. I don't hold that responsibility lightly. It's huge. But, that's the difference. I am truly motivated by taking care of this company and the people within it for the long term."

The Only Way Is Up...?

Elizabeth

Financial controller to owner of her own finance consultancy

Ambition can often get in the way of successful career change. It can muddy the waters of clear-thinking and requires some very honest mirror gazing to unpick the exact motivations underlying an expressed ambition.

Perhaps we set our eyes on a career goal before fully understanding its impacts and consequences? Or we might feel that it would be a waste to throw away a career goal that we have invested fifteen or twenty years chasing. Elizabeth initiated a brutally honest conversation with herself about her ambitions. The results impacted not only her future work but her family relationships, her holidays and unusually her mode of transport!

Her shoulders shimmied along to Strictly Come Dancing's opening titles as she snuggled down for a Saturday night engrossed in fancy footwork. Giggling at their deeply orange skins, squeezed into magnificently sequined, skintight outfits. Guffawing at their attempts to mask their slip-ups.

Tonight, it was Latin night. Her passion.

She challenged the judges aloud and critiqued the form of the professional dancers. Enviously absorbing the intricate cut-outs and every glittering detail of the dresses. Delighting in being in the company of dancers for 90 dazzling minutes.

She had always eschewed the emotional rigidity of the Viennese waltz and foxtrot for the high drama of the Argentine tango.

It was her dance.

When Elizabeth took to the floor, she felt the music and movement light up her insides, from the sheen of her patent toes right up to the perfectly drawn arch of her eyebrows and her sleek, sculpted hair. She felt it connected her to the emotional release button in life.

The stage lights darkened. The first tango performance began.

Her breath almost halted to better absorb their talents for telling stories with their bodies. Assessing their walks, their crosses, their pivots and turns, their figures of eight and those divine leg hooks. Longing to be there herself. To be poured into one of those stunning, daring dresses. To the accompaniment of that marvellous band.

Elizabeth had studied tango for years. Recently she felt it draw her closer into its embrace. Almost clawing inside her skin. But couldn't quite tell why.

Maybe her impending big birthday?

Her transformation into a *very* young grandmother?

Her separation from her partner?

Or perhaps it offered a joyful distraction from her ongoing mental tango with her career?

Over the years she had been promoted by coupling talent and hard work. She had always set her hungry eyes on the number one position in her technical specialism.

She craved control over her own choreography and that of the finance team. She had hankered after the finance director position, the lead dancer, for longer than she could remember.

On the day that an opportunity arose to take over that lead dancer position temporarily, she lunged for it without thinking twice. Legs and arms tense with desire. Willing it to be the performance that would secure the remainder of her career. The dance from which she would retire.

She adored it.

And despised it.

At the same time.

She delighted in the opportunity to kiss one of her career ambitions brazenly on its deeply rouged lips. But the stolen kiss, more of a brief peck in truth, prompted an arched back, a head toss and a sashay off to reconsider if it was in fact her heart's desire.

After the six-month affair with her power position ended, she was forced to decide, was it love or just lust?

She went toing and froing across a slippery, dark dance floor trying to reach the truth.

Was she ready to give up her weekends? To see her perfect posture crumple under work stress and deadlines? Didn't those senior shoes nip a little when she'd worn them through those long days? Didn't the slinky office dress feel a little cool when worn in the office so late at night, and so often?

Oh, but the heady perfume of success and fulfilling a long-held ambition.

The control and the ownership.

The responsibility and respect.

The glory and... that salary. They all certainly smelled magnificent.

But what if she remained as a number two? She would perform and support at her best without all the stress. That would allow her to focus on other life priorities.

Time was needed. Time to rethink the choreography of her life, not just work.

With the savings from her extra pay for that six-month affair, she fled the dance floor. Hung up her Cuban-heeled work shoes and resigned to have a clean break.

And boy, what a break!

A month motorbiking around Europe with her new partner. A month in Scotland with the UK's most renowned tango teachers. A month in Crete and a month in Argentina.

The break reached its finale with Elizabeth performing the Argentine tango in Buenos Aires on her fiftieth birthday. Strictly, a dancing dream come true.

On her return home, she sought out a career coach to put the finishing touches to her toe-dip of a plan, then announced the choreography of the next twenty years to friends and family.

She would set up her own business in finance but with her own style and panache. She would choose her own partners, small businesses, then help them to trip their own light fandango with her financial advice.

She would make sure they pivoted on the right heel, at the right moment. And support them through the lifts and dips of their business lives.

She also discovered little-toed, dancing grandchildren who needed Nana to teach them their moves. Growing upper and older together.

When I met Elizabeth, she was in her second year of running her own accounting business. She was so positive and excited to show me some of the stunning photos from her trip to Buenos Aires, fulfilling one of her life goals. I asked how it felt now to be living the life that her deep searching had uncovered and this is what she said.

> "I feel very, very happy. When I meet up with people who haven't seen me for a long time, they always comment on how well I look. I am sleeping very well and investing time in me and my family.
>
> I have a lovely relationship with my grandchildren because I look after them regularly, which would have been impossible in a full-time role. And I get to do work that I love and am good at. Life is great."

The Experimentalist

Andrea

Corporate career to full-time writer

Sometimes an unexpected exit from a company offers an opportunity to create an experiment to test whether a new career might work. Andrea enjoyed her career and was caught unawares when the company decided to shut down her office. But their decision, followed by her choice to accept the redundancy package, opened a new door for her to conduct a time-limited career change experiment.

Sick child. Childminder stuck at an airport overseas. Two parents working full-time. Andrea had lost the coin toss and watched her husband walk out the front door, heading to the office, daring to smile, relieved at his lucky win, this time.

If she just had a few more hands. Six maybe? Then she could keep all her shows on the road.

Cuddler of the teething baby. Popper of the corn for the movie day the two older children were embarking on. Maker of breakfast, lunch and dinner. Constant water refiller. Wiper-upper of accidents. And chief entertainer.

Then leader of the Monday morning team meeting via phone, a meeting filled with youngsters without kids, coin toss winners and those with childminders who made it to work through the snow. Writer of that report to hand in at the last possible minute this afternoon. And crafter of team appraisals.

Dig deep.

Make it happen.

Like she always did.

One of Andrea's two arms had been filled with the baby since the wee hours, the other the laptop. She floated in a sea of Calpol syringes, teething gels, nasal sprays and tissues. Her brain went into overdrive. Conjuring up thirty-second treasure hunts and hoping they might last for hours. Using reverse psychology to motivate the older child not to argue with the younger. Suggesting games and activities they could do by themselves because when she put the baby down the crying began.

Effort-filled smiles that couldn't stretch to her eyes. Busy begging them to play nicely together while mummy worked. For eight hours.

Nearly broken, by mid-afternoon, she gave up the ghost.

Switched off her laptop and morphed back into an adequate, two-armed mummy again.

Peppa Pig joined the working-from-home party. There were games on the carpet with snuggles and cuddles as prizes. Andrea's shoulders relaxed knowing that tomorrow would be another 200% day to help her recover from the guilt and lost hours of today. But this afternoon was theirs.

86

Late that night, her brain still fizzing from the stress of the day, glass of wine in hand, she was filled with knowing that she couldn't be the only one in the world to feel like this. She googled a search to make sure.

With the exception of her close friends, working mothers seemed to be just making it happen. Beavering away behind the scenes. Calmly juggling all the balls. Spinning all the plates. Walking an effortless tightrope between guilt and high performance.

Radio shows, news interviews, social media articles all seemed only to highlight the have-it-all, do-it-all, easy lifestyle.

Banking goddesses with seven children. Awe-inspiring boss mums on Desert Island Discs being lauded above the rest of our world of successful working women who had been disappeared from the media. They appeared to have swallowed their daily emotions with their voices. To have gulped down their normal feelings of inadequacy.

Andrea wasn't aiming for parenting perfection. She was just trying not to mess the kids up. She didn't aspire to be a perfect boss. Just not to prioritise work above everything else.

Spinning kids, love lives and work was portrayed in the media as just a simple juggling problem. The ordered swapping of one with the other at different times. But that never rang true.

Not talking about this openly or telling the whole truth was making life worse for us all. Perpetuating the myth.

She was inspired to say the unsaids. To expose the true cracks in the have-it-all life. To tell the truths and the whole truths.

The warts and the alls.

Andrea snapped open the laptop again, this time not searching just writing. Nimble thoughts and fast-fingered typing, the words just flew onto the screen. Reciting the things that get said in kitchens all over the Western world but hadn't quite made it to the mass media.

"Just press the bloody button!" she commanded herself again. She had been telling herself this for the last ten minutes after crafting her notes into something that mattered to her and hoping it would matter to others. It was ready, but was it good enough?

Publish? Deep breath.

Click.

Smile.

Spawned from frustration and the lack of anything like it out there, she'd released her fourth bambino into the world.

Words and paragraphs instead of arms and legs. Title and subtitles replaced eyes and ears. Raw emotion in place of the heart.

Her first blog post ever.

After pressing the button, a freedom and lightness emerged. She wanted more of that sort of release.

Writing a few times a month, grew to weekly articles and then increased to any time she felt like it.

Some months later she discovered that her company would be closing her office. A role that she had loved would be gone. The unexpected redundancy offered her a way out and a way in simultaneously. She loved writing so much, but could she make it pay the bills?

Andrea wanted to grasp this once-in-a-lifetime opportunity and use her redundancy package to conduct an experiment. A six-month promise to herself and her family that if it didn't work, she would put her corporate dresses on again.

An unusual chance to create a working life different from anything she'd ever imagined. One where she could use her new voice and this new talent every minute of her working day. She could talk about writing, think about writing and indeed, just write.

A whirlwind of an experiment. Propelled by a hurricane of energy. Five-month-old in tow, she spent every one of his sleeping moments writing, blogging and seeking out paid writing work. Every evening, as the three little ones slept, she continued to write furiously.

Willing it to be possible.

Exhausted and exhilarated, bruised and battered, nervous yet knowing, she drew the six-month line in the sand to an end.

She'd done it!

She'd made it!

She had secured enough regular clients and the promise of ongoing paid articles to cover her half of the bills. She had proved it. A Blog Of The Year award secured it.

The experiment had been fruitful.

She would continue to write for her life... and her living.

I found Andrea's reframing of an unexpected redundancy from work that she really enjoyed into a chance of a lifetime very moving. Her self-awareness drew her to time her experiment to make sure that it was both financially possible *and* that she enjoyed the actual work enough to keep doing it. This style of career change is the opposite of a leap of faith. When we chatted, I was so curious to find out how she feels now, after a few years of full-time writing and several successful, published novels under her belt. See for yourself.

"Amazing! It's amazing every day. I've never had a moment of regret. It feels brilliant!

Of course, it's not brilliant every minute of every day. I will never go back... unless I can't pay the mortgage."

Prising Open the Jar of Secrets

The night of my elder daughter's first birthday, my husband almost died twice.

His parents, brothers and their wives had come to celebrate with us and we'd experimented with a few new Mexican recipes. Twelve hours later, I had experienced a few of my life's firsts.

- Half-carrying my man mountain of a rugby-playing husband, into the accident and emergency department.
- Silently eyeballing a doctor speed off for a second opinion when he couldn't find Phil's blood pressure reading on the third attempt.
- Being escorted by a kind-eyed, soft-voiced nurse into an empty room with a sofa.
- Calling my mother-in-law to ask her to come to the hospital immediately, trying to not panic her but needing her to move very fast.
- Explaining to my, then childless, brother how to change a one-year-old girl's nappy!

More than a decade later, Phil is fitter and healthier than ever although he has an attachment to his heart that makes him beep at most airport scanners. But the whole situation had three memorable impacts on me.

The first—Mexican mole will never pass my lips again as I initially thought I'd poisoned him. The second—tears fill my eyes every time I think about that phone call to his mum. The third—I find it *much* easier not to sweat the small stuff.

But to recognise the small stuff, I had to figure out exactly what *my big stuff* looked like.

I wasn't at all shocked to find that work had made it into *my big stuff* list. I used to be one of only a few people I knew who admitted in public that they loved their work. It had taken me to London, then to Sydney, where I met Phil and made lifelong friends, and back to the UK to the city where we now live and love.

As a Generation Xer, my work forms such a huge part of my life, my identity and my self-esteem. So, when it stopped being as enjoyable as it used to be, it impacted me more than I could ever have imagined. *Not* doing work that I loved started to wear me down and to fade me out, ever so slowly, over many years. To a point where it was time to do something about it.

It took me several years to hit that tipping point... and several more years to figure out what fit... and then a while longer to set it up in a way that works.

But I don't want you to waste another minute of your precious life.

I want you to get there much more quickly.

I'd love to help you get yourself to the situation where your work fits you better and adds to the spice of your life. Where it feels so enjoyable, so deeply satisfying and fulfilling that you might do it for as long as you possibly can, not for as long as you need.

That's why I've introduced you to just a few of the career changers whose experiences of designing more happiness into their work have left such an indelible mark on me—and I hope on you.

But their experiences couldn't be more different—they come from varied backgrounds, industries, disciplines and career starting points. They have assorted appetites for risk, family situations, personalities and financial positions. They also differ in the degree of change required to have the desired impact on their work happiness.

Despite these variations, there are a number of shared secrets which underpin every single one of their happier career change experiences and you will need to apply these secrets to your personal situation before you can embark on your journey towards happier work for yourself.

Have a guess...

If I told you that there are nine secrets to successful career change embedded in each of the stories, how many would you be able to name right now?

Take five minutes and flick through the stories again to jog your memory.

Attempting this tiny challenge, even if you don't write down your responses, will ensure that the secrets connect more deeply with you and give you a higher chance of career change success when you set about it.

1.

2.

3.

4.

5.

6.

7.

8.

9.

Most people I've asked make a very good stab at three or four without breaking a sweat and the record at first reading currently stands at five.

How did you do?

These secrets, when applied to your personal circumstances, will form the rock-solid foundations to building more satisfying, more fulfilling and more enjoyable work into your life.

So, let's prise open that jar of secrets and move you closer to doing just that.

SECTION 3

Rewriting Your
Future Story

The Secret of Tenacity

In the early days, I found myself leaving conversations with these happier career changers in awe of their ability to keep going when the world appeared to be telling them to give up. I was continually bowled over by the number of times they each had picked themselves up, dusted themselves down and tried again.

But after the first ten or so interviews, I grew to expect moments of almost-failure, moments of deep self-doubt, moments of despair or moments of heartbreak as the odds of success veered towards the impossible. But somehow, I knew that even though every single conversation would include these moments, it was their reactions to these awful moments that shone enough light on their dreams to make them a reality.

Their tenacity in the face of adversity was apparent in each of their experiences, but they demonstrated it very differently.

Ges developed creative recipes with baked beans so that they could live off his wife's part-time salary to give him enough time to work on his new idea. Anil anticipated financial adversity by downsizing his family home way before he started searching for his first role within a start-up, knowing that he would have to accept a substantial drop in salary to be considered for such roles.

Kate worked every free hour after finishing her full-time job and putting the children to bed, to learn the art and the business of distilling gin.

Andy continued to work a small, part-time job to keep cash coming in while he promoted his dream every other moment in the gym, at the coffee shop, in the bank and everywhere until the point when he had secured enough clients to work 100% in his own business.

Charlotte's first business failed even though she loved every minute of it. But when her back was right against the wall and her bank balance was screaming at her to go back to a corporate job, she didn't back down. She tweaked her idea and resculpted her business offering one last time. And this time, it worked.

Jennifer swallowed her feelings and went back to work with the same selfish team, who hadn't even wished her well before her major surgery, while she figured out a plan that would allow her to be appreciated for doing work that she loved in the future.

Andrea spent every penny of her redundancy package conducting a once-in-a-lifetime, six-month experiment to see if she could earn enough using her new-found talent to avoid the need to secure another corporate job. She wrote every minute she was awake and her children were asleep.

Clare self-published her book when publishers weren't interested. Then she persisted in attending book fairs where she sold mightily few books, but being there allowed her to connect with a magazine editor who radically changed her fortunes.

I found myself cheering with delight when I heard their stories of tenacity in the face of potential failure. My inner cheerleader was shaking her pom-poms and doing the splits in the air when they each won out over adversity.

They somehow knew or had faith that success sat one half-step beyond the point at which others would give up.

They did not give up.

They were so dedicated to the idea of seeking out happier work, that what others might have called *sacrifices* simply felt like the necessary actions which gave their dream the best possible chance of success.

The Secret of Powerful Vulnerability

As they shared their inspiring stories with me, I found myself falling a little in love with each of them but couldn't put my finger on why for some time. Initially, I figured I was stirred by their relentless commitment to making their dreams a reality.

But no, that wasn't it. Later, I thought perhaps it was their confidence to follow their instincts that wowed me, but the reality was in fact the opposite.

They each possessed a very tangible sense of vulnerability that floored me every time I finished a conversation with them. It transported me back to my own very painful period of vulnerability when I had fallen out of love with my own corporate career and couldn't see a way out.

They each experienced a similar period when they also felt stuck. Stuck either in the wrong job, company or industry or stuck by the absence of a great Plan B.

They each told me their own version of admitting that "I'm somewhere I don't want to be and I don't know how to change it... yet."

Contrary to what they thought might happen by admitting their vulnerability, their worlds did not implode.

The opposite happened.

It freed them from whatever was trapping them. It gave them an opportunity to begin to create the possibility of a new world, without some of the fog that had blurred their vision in the past.

On her hospital bed just before her operation, Jennifer had her moment when she realised that no matter how hard she worked in her company, she would never feel as valued as she needed to feel.

Even though Liz wasn't at all unhappy, she wanted more in her life after her children had left home and to her surprise, bread baking offered her much more than she had ever hoped.

Joanne wanted the ability to switch her mind off at weekends to enjoy family time, but she realised that being an entrepreneur didn't allow that. Nick realised, just in time, that no matter how hard he worked, his values would never connect with the private equity company who had acquired the business.

And David went against old-fashioned, corporate expectations by deciding that he wanted more freedom to spend time with his family.

When Elizabeth made the decision that the finance director role she had been aiming towards for most of her career wasn't for her, she took some time to explore that vulnerable position while motorcycling around Europe and tango dancing in Argentina.

Admitting aloud and accepting their personal vulnerability allowed each of these individuals to look at their work from a completely different angle.

From there, they all took a step forward, backwards or sideways to seek help or learn what they needed to learn to move in a different direction.

Each of these very ordinary, flawed and wonderful human beings have been able to transform what society often perceives as a weakness into a position of great power, freedom and opportunity.

It's no small achievement and that's why I fell in love with each of them, just a little.

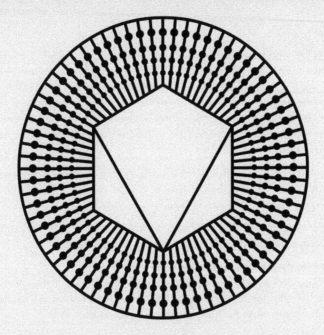

The Secret of Lean, Muscled Adaptability

When we spend a great deal of time within one style of role, one industry or one field, often our powers of adaptability become a little... flabby.

By walking in each of their shoes for even a few minutes you can appreciate how often these individuals needed to adapt themselves, their lifestyles and their work modes in response to their new situations.

Their flabby powers of adaptability soon became lean and strong. In order to become successful in their new careers, they had to learn fast and adapt to what was required.

Charlotte adapted her entire business model, website and brand multiple times to make it commercially sustainable. Clare had to learn the pitfalls of overseas printing after feeling devastated when the shipment of her first book arrived with egg noodles in between her beautifully illustrated pages.

Andy learned to perfect his pitch to potential clients while looking after his few early clients and doing a part-time job until he reached the point where his existing clients became the main source of his new clients. Nick spent his hard-earned savings to allow himself to recover enough to have sufficient energy to experiment with all sorts of new career ideas before an old colleague presented him with the perfect idea.

Julian and Karen had to dive headlong into the world of food production standards before they could sell even one jar of their amazing sauces to the general public.

Andrea had to learn how and who to pitch to in order to find enough regular, paid writing work to allow her to do it full-time.

Their journeys towards doing work that they find more satisfying and fulfilling isn't over. Their worlds will keep changing but their lean, muscled adaptability will keep helping them to react, to rise to the challenges to make the most of their opportunities.

Even if you believe your adaptability muscles have become a little flabby, I can assure you that these individuals were not born with these finely honed muscles. They can be developed like any other skill. They can be whipped into shape in a shorter time than you think.

If you have the motivation, your own adaptability muscles can be sculpted to impressive levels.

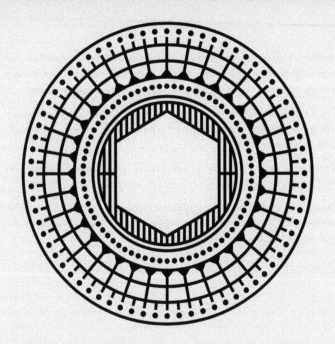

The Secret of Personalising Success

Each of the individuals detached in some way from society's idea of success to create their new, very personal definition.

Their drive to do more fulfilling work was so strong that they were prepared to forgo the elements of their identities that didn't align with their new aim.

For example, Elizabeth let go of her long-held success definition—being on a career path towards finance director—to personalise her new view of success. This time around, she placed more emphasis on lifestyle, health and family goals than she had in the past.

Ges let go of his high-end supermarket idea of success and embraced his new discount shopper identity to allow him to try out his new career idea.

Anil traded in his on-the-path-to-country-leadership definition of success to have more hands-on influence on the growth of a young start-up.

Martine let go of her jet-setting, international HR career to do more personally satisfying HR work locally to be able to be at home most evenings to support her daughters through their teenage years.

We all have definitions of success that link to our identities which often get in the way of allowing us the freedom to do work that might make us happier.

Interestingly, none of these individuals view their new success definitions and the follow-on impacts as *sacrifices*.

Instead, it seemed to me that by consciously personalising their new definitions of success and then taking action, they revelled in the freedom and clarity that it offered them.

The Secret of Big Dreams and Mini Actions

The individuals you have met have grand visions but balance those big dreams with realistic, small, tangible actions every day.

For instance, Julian and Karen dream of transforming the pre-packed sauce aisle in our supermarkets to be tastier without all the nasties. So, each day they wake up and do the small tasks that contribute to their vision, like learning food hygiene standards and the art of jar-labelling.

Kate wakes up every morning to tweak gin recipes, look at new premises, manage staff, pitch to new suppliers—all of which contribute to her dream of creating the finest gin in the world.

David and Elizabeth, who moved into consulting careers, both allocate time each week to networking and deepening their relationships with people who can help them secure their future roles. This allows them to thoroughly enjoy being a very present dad and a motorbike riding, tango dancing grandmother knowing that they are doing everything possible to secure future work.

Lindsay wanted to link quality wine and amazing customer service in a way that her industry doesn't do as well as she'd like, so she spent a great deal of time in the first few years figuring out warehousing problems.

All of them have found that realising their big dreams takes longer than they had hoped. But they strategically researched exactly what was required to make their dreams happen and then broke it down into a series of many smaller actions.

Very often, especially in the early stages of their new career, they work when others are sleeping, partying or relaxing.

They all appeared to clearly understand that their bigger vision requires them to take thousands of the small actions every week that will make their bigger dreams possible.

The Secrets of Kryptonite and Superpowers

From your current situation, these two inseparably linked secrets could have the greatest immediate impact on your career, today.

Kryptonite

Firstly, by getting a crystal-clear understanding of their kryptonite, these individuals consciously defined their new work boundaries.

Kryptonite is the word I use to describe the factors that hinder or potentially destroy the chances of making our work more deeply satisfying. It is rarely one element but a very personal combination of some of the following—close working personalities, leadership styles, cultures, working styles and environments that no longer fit.

To give you some examples, Duncan's kryptonite was the cultural short-term thinking of big corporations, but he could withstand it while he searched for the right small business to invest in for his long term.

Andy's kryptonite combined the futility and lack of interest in real value creation that he experienced in listed businesses. When he hit his tipping point, even though he had no idea what to do next, he *knew* with certainty that he couldn't expose himself to his kryptonite any longer without devastating results.

Charlotte's kryptonite revolved around the dullness of working without creativity and, according to her partner, that absence had begun to wash the colour from her entirely.

Nick felt weakened by the leadership style of his business' new owners while the never-ending working style of being an entrepreneur had begun to have a kryptonite effect on Joanne's work happiness.

Jennifer's kryptonite turned out to be a culture of profit over people and the lack of appreciation from co-workers.

Karen didn't acknowledge her kryptonite, the political dance required to be successful in her head teacher role, until it had almost broken her.

Even if it took time to get there, they each defined their future boundaries more clearly than they had in the past. They spent time to get to a clear list of what would get in the way of their happier working future and then they moved on.

Superpowers

Some of the individuals you've met had a vague idea of their superpowers but often in the process of considering and researching their Plan B, their superpowers became more obvious.

I use the term *superpowers* to mean the very specific personal skills that make us feel brilliant when we use them, the unique specific talents that we can't stop using, the abilities that others often appreciate more than we do because we find them easy and the aptitudes that we could use all day without feeling drained.

Knowing their superpowers allowed them to choose the right business model for them. Which is why Martine chose the franchise model to give her support in the areas she wasn't as strong in, so that she could free up her time to concentrate on using her superpowers. Karen and Julian designed their working partnership around business activities that allowed them to focus on each of their superpowers. And Charlotte chose her customer base around her superpowers.

Ges very tightly designed his public speaking business around his new-found but long-standing superpower. While Clare reinstated an almost forgotten superpower in the illustration of her children's book, incorporating elements of design and fashion.

And Liz unveiled a completely new baking-related superpower and combined it with an existing talent for teaching individuals new skills, in a way certain to ensure her business success.

Whether these people consciously designed their business around their specific superpowers or used their superpowers to work in their preferred way, they all defined themselves as happier using their talents more often than in previous work scenarios.

Of course, none of these individuals are using their superpowers every moment of every day, but the more they use their superpowers, the happier they appeared to become.

The Secret of Conscious Planning

There is a flawed general belief that career change happens in one linear step. That one day you are a lawyer and the next you are a mega-successful beer entrepreneur.

Not a single one of these individuals, or any of the others I have met, took a blind leap into the unknown with their fingers crossed, hoping. They all created a plan, in their own personal style.

Lindsay sits at one end of the spectrum by spending an entire year investigating her new industry to come up with her very credible business plan. Whereas Kate spent one leg of a long commute pulling together her rough business plan and then evolved it as she learned along her journey.

Anil understood that he needed to make himself attractive to start-ups, so he manoeuvred his experience over several years to make that possible. Whereas Charlotte was already spending her weekends getting to know the passionate, new food brand owners who ultimately became her paying clients.

Duncan knew he would own a business one day, but downsized while he investigated lots of potential businesses to make sure he was in a position to buy his perfect business when it presented itself to him.

Ges had spent a large part of his spare time over the years fine-tuning his rare public speaking skills, volunteering at charity events, presenting training courses at work and hosting events. This meant he could hit the ground running and had lots of relevant contacts when he decided to turn his talent into his new career.

Liz offered her time for free, doing dishwashing and other menial jobs in kitchens, to learn as much as she could from professional chefs, so that she could design her new work in a way that would suit her.

There were zero leaps of faith and zero leaps into the unknown.

It took time and research. It took commitment to try out new ideas and perform mini experiments. It involved analysis at each step to understand exactly which elements fit and which didn't. It involved lots of learning.

They each locked in the pieces of their happier work jigsaw, piece by piece. In a very conscious way.

Each piece of the jigsaw led them closer to work that would play to their talents and their ambitions. Work that would suit their resources and their personalities. Work that would ultimately create opportunities for themselves to perform happier work than they had done in the past.

The Secret of First-step Bravery

Bravery isn't required when you have nothing to lose. But all of these individuals had much to lose.

Beyond commitments to their partners, families and mortgage companies, many feared personal failure after achieving success in their earlier careers. Yet, as we know, they understood that society's definition of success no longer aligned with their personal success definition.

Even though they had each taken the necessary time to figure out their personalised definition of success, they were still afraid of failure.

Yet, they all appeared to have a moment when their fear of failure was trumped by their fear of living the next twenty years doing work that didn't satisfy or fulfil them.

So, they took the first step.

The scariest step.

The loneliest step

The bravest step.

For Charlotte, that meant deciding that she would not remain in her role whether her name was on the redundancy list or not. For Ges, that meant employing a career coach to help him see his career from a totally different angle.

Karen's first step was resigning from the role that was eroding her health. Andrea's first step was to agree with her husband the time frame for her writing experiment to either succeed, or for her to return to corporate life.

David's first step was to ask a respected colleague her opinion on his situation. Elizabeth's first step was to take a break from her career to do some serious thinking about her next moves. And Nick's was simply to agree with himself that his future was elsewhere.

These first steps required dig-deep courage.

These individuals changed the course of their careers, and in many cases their lives, by taking one brave step.

That first brave step then spawned thousands of other mini steps which required far less bravery.

Then they continued to take mini steps forwards, sideways and sometimes backwards to allow them to venture into their futures— their happier working futures.

One Moment, One Choice

Can you keep doing what you are doing for another ten or twenty years?

If you answered "No!", *THIS MOMENT* is the right time to start figuring out what you'll do instead.

You now know from this wonderful collection of normal, yet so inspiring, individuals, that doing happier work is a choice. A choice made in one brave moment.

Make this your moment.

Whatever sparks of inspiration or flashes of insight you felt while sharing their experiences, use them to fuel your bravery to take your first step.

Start... today... RIGHT NOW!

1. Write down today's date on the first page of this book

You will want to remember today. Today was the day you began to design happier work for yourself.

Not the day you resigned. Not the day you decided upon the finer details of your future. The day you made a commitment to yourself to make more fulfilling and satisfying work one of your life's top priorities.

2. Name and shame your kryptonite

Make a list of the very specific elements of your work that you would like a great deal less of in your future.

You'll have this list nailed in no time because you've been thinking about these elements for a while. You've probably been complaining about them to your nearest and dearest for some time. They are on the tip of your tongue, I know it.

Once you release them, they will begin to lose some of their power and allow you to open your mind to changes, however small, to reduce their negative grip on you.

3. Make it your mission to seek out individuals who describe themselves as "happy in their work"

Ask friends, family and strangers for recommendations. Then pick their brains on how they made that happen.

Quiz them as to how they ended up doing what they are doing, how they made it fit them, which parts of their work they really enjoy and anything else that you are curious about. I can assure you that they will be flattered by your interest in them and blown away by your vulnerability.

Begin today by sharing in the experiences of lots of other individuals like you who are a little further down their journey towards happier work on my website (www.midlifeunstuck.com).

I assure you that once you discover a few of them, you'll begin to come across people who are loving their work everywhere. In just one week, I chatted to one in the florist, another in a coffee shop and yet another while watching my daughters do gymnastics.

4. Nail your numbers

Financial commitments played a big part in the journeys to doing happier work for all of these individuals and I guarantee it will in yours too.

In my experience, it is one of the biggest hindrances to designing happier work but it always surprises me how few people I work with can quote their exact minimum monthly outgoings.

If finances could get in the way of you doing more satisfying work, knowing in detail where your money disappears to every month will prompt changes that will give you more options.

You can then make decisions today that might stop you blaming finances as the reason you are still in the same spot in five years!

5. Begin to unveil your potential superpowers

For almost everyone I have worked with, this was a difficult task. But, done well, it will give you the crucial corner pieces in your happier work jigsaw. It might take some time and quite a few attempts but be tenacious.

Take a piece of paper, split it into four equal sections. In the first section, write a long list of the things that you do that others compliment you on. In the second section, list the activities that you really enjoyed at any point over the course of your career. In the third section, list the activities in or out of work that you simply cannot stop doing. In the fourth square, write a detailed list of things that you really enjoy helping others to do.

Within this one full page of notes, there will be some patterns and some running themes that with a little analysis will help you recognise some of your superpowers. That analysis generally takes me a morning or an afternoon of talking through with a client to nail down a specific list of personal superpowers, but you will be able to get a good indication from answering these questions.

Once you have a tighter grasp on the specifics behind your personal superpowers, you will have in your hands the confidence-enhancing, golden nuggets upon which to begin designing the detail behind your future happier career.

What I Know for Sure...

Once you have completed these five activities, you will have begun a journey with no return.

You will have dug deep to take your own first brave step into your happier working future, a working future in which you do work that matters more to you.

Anything you do beyond these first few steps won't be anywhere near as scary—they will be just mini steps and mini experiments.

Because, what I know for sure is, that your life *will* be too short to keep wasting your precious time doing work that isn't making you happy.

About Lucia

Stories have always fascinated and inspired me. The stories I heard as a child moved me, challenged me and drove me to enjoy working in various corporate roles around the world.

It is not always the big, dramatic stories that capture my attention. As a shy little girl I loved being in the back seat of the car while my mum and her friends revealed the hidden details of small-town life in Northern Ireland to one another.

Then, I gradually realised that there were unspoken tales—of motivation, of fear, of sadness, of joy. These hidden layers were to play an increasingly important role in my life and the lives of those

I worked with in corporate. Today they are at the heart of my work with my fellow Gen Xers.

I spent many years listening to the career stories of senior leaders from different companies, industries and countries. In the ten years leading up to my own change of career, I listened to more than 3,500 career stories as I helped to find them new positions. Gradually I realised that the frustrations, hopes and regrets they shared were no longer going to be satisfied with a simple swap to another position with the same problems.

This happened to me too after twenty years in similar roles but at increasingly senior levels.

I needed to change. To rewrite my future tale of work and life. To tap into my Gen X fire and claim my own mission to eradicate mid-career unhappiness. It wasn't easy, it took time and focus and a willingness to escape the safe straightjacket of the corporate world. Just like most of the people I now work with.

Now I get to love helping Gen Xers review, rewrite and retell their own career and life stories. Their stories now move me, challenge me and drive me to seek out those who are beginning their walk of freedom, their mid-career revolution.

If your own story doesn't fascinate or inspire you anymore then it is time to rewrite it.

You can access many resources and find out more about how I can help you personally with your own transformation at:

www.midlifeunstuck.com

mPowr Titles

Speak Performance

Ges Ray

ISBN—978-1-907282-87-4

For those afraid of speaking in front of a small team, groups of strangers or large crowds. How to be a confident, compelling and convincing speaker.

When Fish Climb Trees

Mel Loizou

ISBN—978-1-907282-85-0

For those who are fed up of quick-fix solutions in the workplace and who want rich, productive relationships and results which flow from affirming values.

Storyselling

Martyn Pentecost

ISBN—978-1-907282-59-1

For those who wish to go beyond simplistic hero—problem— resolution approaches to storytelling and business. How to become a master storyseller by exploring ancient storytelling tradtions and contemporary technological innovations.

Your Slides Suck!

David Henson

ISBN—978-1-907282-78-2

For all speakers who need to show information visually. How to make engaging, empowering and effective PowerPoint presentations.

Write Your Book
Grow Your Business

Richard Hagen

ISBN—978-1-907282-54-6

For consultants, trainers, entrepreneurs and busines experts who want to write a book to grow your business. How to avoid the most dangerous pitfalls and set yourself up for maximum succcess before you start to write.

DARE:
Domestic Abuse Rescue Essentials

Diana Onuma

ISBN—978-1-907282-87-92-8

For those facing situations of domestic abuse and those supporting others through these challenges. How to claim your freedom when the need to leave overcomes the reasons to stay.

Lightning Source UK Ltd.
Milton Keynes UK
UKHW020634240519
343261UK00005B/234/P

9 781907 282904